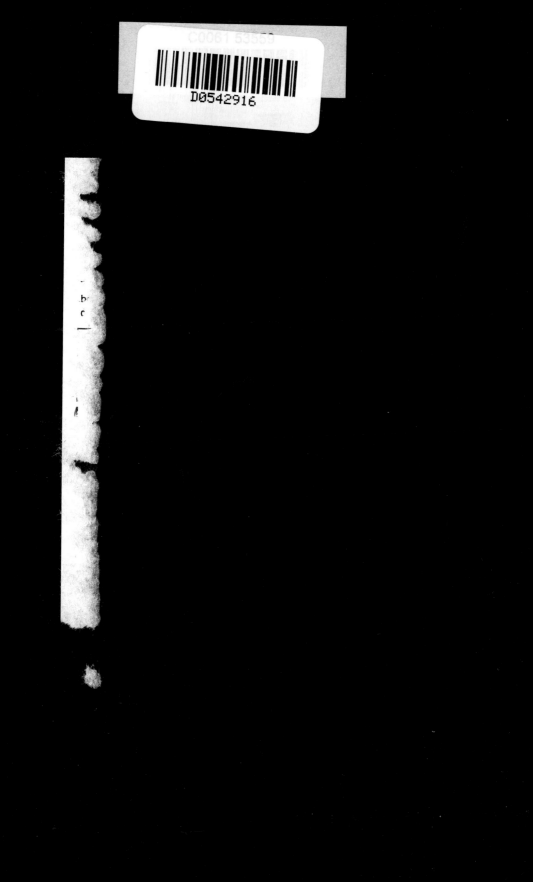

LUCKY

PROFESSOR GREEN
LUCKY

STEPHEN MANDERSON

BLINK
bringing you closer

Published by Blink Publishing
107–109 The Plaza,
535 King's Road,
Chelsea Harbour,
London SW10 0SZ

www.blinkpublishing.co.uk
facebook.com/blinkpublishing
twitter.com/blinkpublishing

978-1-910536-32-2

A CIP catalogue of this book is available from the British Library.

Jacket design by Aidan Cochrane
Typeset by www.envydesign.co.uk
Printed and bound by Clays Ltd, St Ives Plc

1 3 5 7 9 10 8 6 4 2

Text copyright © Stephen Manderson, 2015

All imges © Stephen Manderson uness therwise stated.

Papers used by Blink Publishing are natural, recyclable products made
from wood grown in sustainable forests. The manufacturing processes
conform to the environmental regulations of the country of origin.

Every reasonable effort has been made to trace copyright holders of
material reproduced in this book, but if any have been inadvertently
overlooked the publishers would be glad to hear from them.

Blink Publishing is an imprint of the Bonnier Publishing Group

www.bonnierpublishing.co.uk

TAKE YOUR *LUCKY* EXPERIENCE
BEYOND THE PRINTED PAGE...

Professor Green's *Lucky* Mix Tape app allows you, the reader, to fully immerse yourself in the behind-the-scenes world of Professor Green. From crazy tour bus shenanigans and exclusive never-seen-before footage, to intimate video-logs of some of Professor Green's biggest shows, find out what really happens in the life of Professor Green and what goes on behind the closed doors of one of the world's biggest rap stars.

Download the free app from the iTunes App Store or Google Play Store, point your device at the pages with the Mix Tape icons on them and the exclusive videos and photo galleries will be revealed on the device's screen. Here you will get the chance to see Professor Green's personal videos and unique travelogues, as well as access photographs of the musician as you've never seen him before!

The *Lucky* Mix Tape App requires an Internet connection to be downloaded and can be used on iPhone, iPad or Android devices. For direct links to download the app and further information, visit www.blinkpublishing.co.uk.

CONTENTS

INTRODUCTION

S cared. Scared shitless. It's hardly the first time in my life I've felt this feeling and my enemy is a familiar one – a blank page. Only this time it's not a song I've got to write but a book.

Even when I've done that I still face a task that's almost as difficult – reading it back, when I find that I have a new set of worrying questions. Have I missed anything? Definitely. Is it funny? Subjective. Can readers hear my annoying whiny voice? Well, can you? And are readers asking, Does he put himself down as a form of self-defence? Probably – and what kind of wanker refers to himself in the third person?

I haven't written my story before because of just these sorts of questions. Wondering how I can write it but not over-write it, trying to obey rules of grammar while still writing the same way I talk in conversation. Sometimes I have trouble writing 16 bars of a song – now I have the task of filling all these pages.

Where do I start? My humble beginnings in Hackney? My aims and aspirations? My love for potatoes and my hatred of cheese? How about my once-keen interest in horticulture? Oh, and then there's the music.

I released my first mixtape in March 2006. *Lecture #1* included a preview of 'Before I Die', a song which listed all the things I wanted to accomplish at the time; some goals more serious than others. Things were looking good for me. I had just been signed to The Beats Recordings, run by The Streets' Mike Skinner and I was full of ambition.

I've since ticked off a few of those aims. I've had the No 1 single and in 2009 I finally got my teeth straightened. I've been to Amsterdam and I have a car with massaging seats. I haven't driven a Ferrari but I've had some pretty nice cars, as well as a driving ban as a result of chasing after a little shit who'd nicked my watch and was threatening Millie, once my girlfriend and now my wife. What else? There may or may not have been a few pairs of fake boobs but I will admit I didn't get around to withdrawing a million pounds in £1 coins from Barclays just for the sake of it. I did almost get killed. That was when I was attacked by a random punter I'd only brushed past in a club. He stabbed me in the neck through the tattoo that says 'Lucky'. Thinking about it now, I've probably had an even wilder ride than I thought I might have when I wrote that song.

The Beats label didn't last long and when it folded I was almost back where I started, making music without making money from it and supporting myself through dealing. It was very far from where I wanted to be but I'm not going to gloss over that. I'm going to be honest in talking about every aspect of my life. I've always been open about my past and I'm going to continue to do so. For a start, being honest means I'm not vulnerable to newspapers pulling skeletons out of my closet. Most of the things I've got up to that I probably shouldn't have I've written about in my lyrics. And I'll always stand by my words.

The tough times that followed my first glimmers of success were perhaps a better foundation than they seemed at the time. Maybe without having to rely on myself I wouldn't have met Lily Allen and recorded 'Just Be Good to Green', the song that kick-started the second and – so far – longer-lasting part of my career. I've since gone on to release three albums, a succession of hit songs and I've had a TV series following part of the journey. I'm not sure that's something I would have predicted when I started out rapping with my mates on the blocks in east London. I've travelled the world, played to stadium crowds, at festivals, won awards and performed live on TV shows – not to mention been interviewed on *Loose Women*.

More recently I've started to use my voice for something beyond my own profit by highlighting the often neglected subject of mental health. But there are those who would rather ignore the achievements and focus on what they don't like about me because I'm a rapper. Water off a duck's back. A lot of people just don't understand the art of the MC – the wordplay. Rappers communicate an emotion. They're telling stories, drawing from their experiences and making art. Focusing on a few bad words is just one way of avoiding the real problems that can be expressed in rap.

For a long time before I was successful all I did was what I had to do to survive. I didn't have the necessary guidance to make it through school without dropping out and I had anxiety that crippled me at times – and still does; I fight it on a daily basis. I had a day job for a long time and I supplemented that with dealing and that was how I made the music work.

I've been extremely fortunate to have the friends I've made. They were like the family I never quite had. Most of my friends then are my friends now.

I get to work with some incredibly creative people and there's been plenty of good times on tour and in the studio. Sometimes my career has accelerated too quickly to think about, let alone document. I'm probably best known for my work with Emeli Sandé on 'Read All About It', the song that gave us both our first No 1 and ignited our careers.

This is the first time I've tried to document the goings-on over the years, the trouble with school, the dealing, the depression, the music and the marriage. Have I been lucky? If I have, I've had to make all the luck for myself. I didn't have parents to guide me when I was growing up and although my nan took that role, it was still hard not to have a mum and dad who were there all the time. By the time I was ready to reach out to my dad to try and make some of that better, it was too late. I lost him before I got the chance to know him, and to find out why he was hardly ever around.

It would take me a long time, a lot of late nights and a smidgen of naughty behaviour before I found a settled relationship that was unlike most examples of relationships I had been exposed to growing up. Now I've got something loving and lasting – which began with a petrol station and a particular *FHM* cover on the shelves featuring a certain somebody in a pair of socks and not much else. At a time that is now so transitional and full of reflection it makes perfect sense to try and create some record of what took place while I still remember, as fragmented as some of the memories may be.

Having waited till it was too late to say what I wanted to say my father, I'd just like to thank my nanny Pat: I love you. I only hope I'm not too much of an embarrassment and, if I am, that you forgive me. Without you and Nanny Edie I wouldn't be the man I am today – I hope I'm one you can be proud of.

NORTHWOLD

A lot is made of where you come from in hip-hop. It's true of garage and grime too, but it goes back to hip-hop – and before that the blues. Biggie was from Bed-Stuy, Jay-Z from the Marcy Projects, Nas from the Queensbridge Houses, Task Force are from the Highbury estate, Wretch 32 is from the Tiverton estate in Tottenham, Wiley and Dizzee are from Bow and me, I'm from the Northwold estate, Clapton, London. Four stories tall, 459 flats, built before World War II. No different to any number of estates around London.

I've been to New York – Brooklyn, Queens and the Bronx. The Projects seem just like the blocks in Clapton – they don't look too bad on a quiet afternoon. But appearances can hide secrets. I grew up in Clapton and it was my world for many years. It was full of my people – friends, and maybe a few enemies – and it left me a legacy. When I started out in music I had no other perspective to write from because I didn't know anything else. Those American rappers probably thought their records would only be bought locally or maybe reach the rest of New York and the East Coast. Suddenly they were selling hundreds of thousands around the world and kids in London knew the name of the block they were born in. I learned all those names and heard the legends built around them from their songs – but in the end they're still just buildings. It was the musicians that gave them meaning.

I was born on 27th November 1983 in Bart's hospital in east London. My mum, Lynn, was just 16 when she had me and there are only a few photos of mum, dad and me together: a couple from the hospital before I was taken home and one or two outside in the estate or at the homes of other family members. Peter, my dad, left my mum for another girl not long afterwards.

Mum lived with her mother, my nan Patricia, who has looked after me from day one. She was there all throughout labour and although the nurses sent her out when my dad arrived, he left again and a nurse let her back in. Nan saw me being born and she was the one who first held me: she says that my mum was just so young that the nurse automatically gave me to her instead. That nurse had the right instinct. My mum wasn't old enough to carry the responsibility of looking after a child. She wanted to be out with her mates, not staying home with the baby.

We lived at No 1 Wentwood House on the Northwold estate. My granddad originally took on the property as the caretaker although he'd left my nan by the time I was born. Somehow our three-bed flat accommodated six of us – me, my nan, my mum, her brothers Mark and Paul, who were 20 and 18 and my nan's mother, Edie. From my earliest days Edie had a soft spot for me and I loved her to bits. Nan looked after her as well as caring for me.

Nan worked as a cleaner and Paul was doing an apprenticeship at a building firm. Nanny Edie and Mark looked after me when they weren't around. Mark, who was unable to work because of epilepsy, soon learned how to change my nappies and feed me just as a father would. Nan and Edie took the night shift, between them juggling changes of clothes and bottles – I had never been breast-fed as Mum wasn't around to do it. I was on Cow and Gate powdered milk that came in tins instead and as Nan received benefits she had to get vouchers which she'd take to the doctors to get the milk.

When I cried at night, Nan later said, I would wake everyone up except my mum and although Nan was laughing when she said it, it was true. But it didn't matter as it wasn't as if my mum lived with us for long anyway. She moved out before I was a year old, long before I could have any recollection of her being there all the time. Yet she didn't drop out of my life in the way that my dad had. She was always around the flat but still I bonded with my dad from an early age, perhaps because I wanted what I really couldn't have from him – his presence.

Paul moved out some years later at the age of 24. I remember his girlfriend Karen – later his wife – was always very nice to me as a kid. She would always buy me presents; I would often get little boxes of Lego from her and sweets. I recently found out while talking to her about writing this book and digging for some info this was purely to try and distract me so she could shag my uncle – I suppose she can be forgiven, she was only 17.

With Paul and my mum no longer living there, the flat was then home to four of us but that was enough – it was still crowded. Nanny Edie slept on an armchair in the living room that folded out into a bed. One of my earliest memories is being woken up and walked by my nan to the dining room where my birthday cake was. I even remember the pyjamas I was wearing. There's a photo of me and my cake and the candles, all two of them. I had curly hair as a kid and I was very blond – I could have passed for Scandinavian or perhaps Polish. That blond. My nan put me in for the *Hackney Gazette* cute kiddies competition when I was four but early stardom eluded me. It didn't matter to Nan and her friends who swear that I was a little angel back then, although I remember often being called less complimentary things than a 'little angel'.

Upper Clapton, in particular Northwold, was a tight community. I remember one of the first times I was allowed out in the estate and away from my nan's watchful eye, I ended up with the kids in the swing park by the youth centre in the middle of the estate. I bumped into Mark Warren, whose dad owned the greengrocer where my dad worked when I was born. 'You're Peter's son,' he said. 'I knew you before you were born.' Back then the estate was a big place and I suppose it gave me a sense of security and belonging to know there were people who'd look out for me. As kids, friends would get jobs at the butchers, the fishmonger or the grocer – all on Upper Clapton Road.

But there were problems, sometimes simply a result of so many people living on top of each other and that meant it wasn't fun and games all the time. I walked out of the front door one day and saw half a bunk bed come hurtling down from the balcony above. They'd decided it was easier to throw it over than walk down two flights of stairs and put it by the bins. A few seconds earlier and it would have hit my head before it reached the ground. My nan ran out and went mental at the idiots upstairs. Things could get a bit vocal, let's say, both in our flat and between neighbours even over minor provocations.

There were also the usual stresses that came with living in a council flat, such as reoccurring damp and the rotting wallpaper that came with it, often as a result of broken pipes, poor workmanship and exposure to the great outdoors. In our case the damp was usually caused by the upstairs neighbours who didn't have a shower and instead stood in the bath and filled buckets with water to pour over themselves. The water went everywhere, but mainly through cracks in the flooring, soaking our ceilings and walls. Boilers broke and we had to use the kettle to boil water for baths. I can still remember vividly the Calor gas heaters we all had in our living rooms and the clicks they made as you'd light them, the lino we had on our kitchen floors and, of course, woodchip wallpaper – and the hours it took to strip it off using only an iron for the steam and a stripping knife.

It was harder for many people when there weren't that many jobs, particularly in the years after Margaret-fucking-Thatcher. Some options were simply closed off and others opened up. Options like robbing houses and stealing cars, that kind of thing. When I was older there was an occasion when I saw a couple of friends screaming into the estate in a red Metro with the police right behind them. One was caught almost instantly while the other ran along the balcony shouting, 'You can't catch me!' He ran up some stairs, along the balcony, climbed over the railings, then lowered himself off the edge and hang-dropped down to the floor below. The scum did catch him though. There was a lot more mischief that took place: a Halloween when cars were tipped over by every entrance of the flats and the swing park was set on fire. The electricity was regularly turned off as the keys to the outside electricity cupboards had been stolen by older kids from the nearby council building. Bin chutes were regularly set on fire (the community centre once accidentally caught fire because of burning bins); on one occasion someone's mum got hit in the head with a sling shot; there was a lady who on the estate used to look after the tearaways – people would often hide there if the police had warrants on them. The estate very much belonged to the people in it: what went on in the estate was dealt with in the estate, for the most part.

I wasn't exposed to much crime but it was always there in the background, along with the noise of cars passing over the speed bump directly outside my bedroom wall, noise from the neighbours upstairs, blazing domestics in the estate and the distant sound of the overground trains. Sirens were a regular part of the soundtrack. My first encounter with the roads was when I saw an ambulance tear through the estate, right past our kitchen window. It was headed for someone it turned out I knew, who finished the day in hospital having been bottled and stabbed. Luckily, one of us youngers, a friend of mine, Campbell, ran to the phone box and called an ambulance for him and he later checked himself out of hospital... only to go back and deal with the person who'd had him rushed.

There was a more fateful day when shots rang out nearby on Rossington Street that resulted in the death of a neighbour who was a son of a friend of my family. At that time Hackney was known as the place where you were more likely to hear gunshots than anywhere else in the UK. Shootings took place in broad daylight and there were countless attacks in or around

Chimes nightclub, one of the most popular venues in the area by Lea Bridge roundabout, not far from Clapton station. I often used the underpass before it was eventually decommissioned and cemented up as a result of all the violence.

The High Road became known as 'Murder Mile'. The *Hackney Gazette* was full of crimes that took place on our doorstep every week and there was a long list of things that went unreported. Awful things happened to too many people, good as well as bad, and you just had to live with it. So, as kids, that's what we did and it was these goings on that later provided the inspiration for tracks such as 'Upper Clapton Dance' and 'Jungle'.

One day Nan went to court to make a formal application to take custody of me. Mum was going to fight the custody bid, but my dad was on Nan's side. She won and the court granted her what was called 'care and control' until I was 18. My dad made one of his infrequent appearances when he came to pick up Nan for the hearing. As he arrived I hid from him. He and my nan left, he shouted, 'Bye, Stephen,' and I shouted back, 'Bye, Peter.' Not 'Dad'. Even at that age I knew there was something pretty wrong with our relationship. The truth was I felt scared when he turned up. I had run away in order to protect myself because I knew from experience that as soon as he'd left, I'd cry.

My dad's new partner and mother of his second and third children, Joyce, was a very jealous woman and I sensed that she didn't like competition for Peter's attention. For long periods of my childhood I didn't get to see my dad at all and even when he did turn up his visits were unpredictable and he would soon disappear. One birthday he bought me a battery-powered quad bike. As usual, he delivered the toy and then not long after left again. It was a pretty expensive present, but the cost meant nothing. Spending time with him, on his own, was what I wanted more than any extravagant gift but I never had much chance of that.

He took me to Hamley's toy store when I was four and what I remember most clearly is standing at the top of Regents Street, holding my dad's hand and waiting to cross the road. It'd been the day of the great storm – 15 October 1987 – and the wind in central London, even that afternoon, was tearing through the streets; later, a tree would come down in the flats.

It was a pattern. I wouldn't see my dad for a week at first and then that week would become two weeks, that two weeks would become a month and that month would become a year. Looking back on it as an adult I can understand now perhaps this was to do with his own anxiety – when he did come around he would have my nan to answer to, not just a child who was too young to understand quite what was going on. I don't think he had a great relationship with Paul, either – both my uncles found it hard to look kindly on the situation, not least because they'd had it done to them by their own dad. After 18 months or so of not hearing from Dad it would be Nanny Edie who would get in touch. For a while my dad shared a place with a friend called Ken and she would have to write to Ken and get him to pass the message on.

After the custody hearing I'd see Mum almost every Saturday and Dad not so much. Nan and Edie raised me between them and passed on values such as humility and taught me the good manners that had been so important in their own lives. Nan was so strong in keeping us all together. There aren't many people who'd raise someone else's child single-handed, let alone after raising three of their own and at the same time as caring for their own mother.

A lot of the time Nan had to do three jobs just to keep us going and once, when Edie was ill and I was off school, she took me with her on her cleaning shifts at the banks in town. We were picked up by her boss – it was 4 am, so there was no other way of getting there – and taken up to central London, to the Strand and Clerkenwell Road, where she got to work on her hands and knees cleaning the floors in those huge, echoing buildings. It was dark, deserted and weird and I still recall the almost stale smell and how empty those places were before the day began. And then, when she was done there, she went on to the next job. But Nan never complained, she just got on with things and did the best she could for all of us.

The other pillar of my childhood was Edie. She was central to my life at home, not least because of all the time that my nan spent working. Edie was always around, usually in the living room, so any time I was up and out of my room I'd be with her. She'd always have a smile, always be ready to make me and my friends a hot Ribena or something to eat. Even though we weren't well off and didn't have much, she'd go out of her way to make my friends welcome and she'd let me get up to all sorts. Nan says that I had Edie wrapped around my little finger and there'd be times when Nan would come in after a long day and be angry because I'd messed the place up while she was out. Edie would just say, 'He's a kid. What do you expect?'

That was far from their only disagreement. I wasn't aware of it then but most of the adult relationships in my family were complicated in some way or other. Even as my nan cared for her mother on a daily basis, I remember arguments involving Edie's son, my nan's brother, Billy. He was a grown man and yet she would give him money from her pension. My nan was the one out grafting and putting food on the table while her brother was a gambler, so that was never easy. And in turn my mum didn't have a great relationship with my nan – her own mother. It would take me years to realise how difficult all of this was for everyone. It's only recently that I've begun to realise that my mum had her own problems and things that she probably hasn't dealt with.

My own connection with Edie was far more straightforward. It's thanks to her that I developed a wide vocabulary and love of words. In the mornings before the cartoons came on, when the only thing on the TV was the test card featuring the little girl with the blackboard and her creepy clown, I would snuggle up with her in her chair and we'd read stories to each other, taking it in turns to read a page. I remember vividly the blue blanket she had. I'd climb under it and we'd read together. They're some of my best memories; she made learning fun. Thanks to her, Nan and Mark, I was a keen learner later at school. If there was something I didn't know, I'd want to work it out and if I knew the answer to something I'd put my hand up. I was a nerd. My school reports included comments such as: 'Stephen's mental arithmetic is excellent' and 'Stephen reads fluently and clearly and is accurate. He likes reading more than writing. He should improve his handwriting.'

But I was also an anxious, vulnerable child and found it very difficult to stick at things. I kept taking time off school until, by the time I got to secondary, the effect was so bad that I finished my educational career without sitting a single exam. There was nobody to drag me to school kicking and screaming when I didn't want to go. I changed primary schools more than once because of those attendance problems and it got worse later. It was only ever down to me bunking off – I got on well with the other kids and was never bullied and I didn't have any difficulties coping with school, when in attendance.

Nan and Edie knew how hard it was for me so they were never too stern. Nan later said she thought my truancy had its roots in my parents walking out. She told me that she felt I was thinking that I 'might come home from school one day and we wouldn't be there. You know, my mum and myself. That's how I feel that you were. You felt, Oh, everybody's leaving me.' She realised how much I was hurting but despite all her love there was nothing she could do about that parent-shaped hole in my life.

I would often say that I wanted to stay off school because I didn't feel well. Feeling ill was the only way I could vocalise the crippling anxiety which was something I was too young to understand and didn't have the vocabulary to explain. I wasn't able to express what was going on either to Nan or the doctors, that my emotions would settle in my stomach. I felt them as a physical pain, a knot. That's where I experienced my feelings and the doctors carried out tests in a hunt for physical symptoms, even going so far as sending cameras down my throat to see what was making me ill so often. In the end I was diagnosed with irritable bowel syndrome. I couldn't tell them it was stress back then and although I can talk about emotions now, I feel the result of pressure in the same place; it still goes straight to my gut. While some of the time I was only faking illness to miss school – and Nan knew it – I did spend a lot of time at the doctor's surgery and even if the source wasn't physical, it was debilitating in a very real way. I've still got problems with my health – in 2013 my current doctor was a guest at my wedding, which gives you an idea of how often I see him. I'm still prone to stress-related anxiety.

Physically, I could be a clumsy child and had accidents that resulted in more time away from education. I was forever doing myself some mischief, highlights including running backwards into a pillar at a club during the school holidays and on another occasion running, tripping over and head-butting the floor. I racked up further head injuries and was concussed more than once. Then there was the time I did a forward-roll on the sofa and took my front teeth out on the wooden arm. The dentist put me under with gas that affected me really badly. I came round feeling dizzy and sick and on return visits the staff had to hold me down because I'd kick and fight and punch rather than sit in the dreaded chair. They'd use gas for every tiny little fucking thing. I hated the dentist and suffered nightmares with my teeth rather than go. I never got a brace and my teeth became increasingly crowded and bent. You can see the damage in my early music videos.

Accidents kept me off school some of the time but I quickly bounced back from the bumps and scrapes. And even serious illnesses didn't keep me down for long. But anxiety and depression would stop me in my tracks. They were the hardest to shift and that hasn't changed. All of the days I'd take off school due to my anxiety meant I had hard questions to face when I went back in but I didn't know how to answer them. Even when I hadn't been off sick, kids wanted answers to questions that I couldn't give and they unwittingly contributed to my anxiety.

'Why's your mum so old?'

'Erm… she's not my mum, she's my nan.'

'Why are you with your nan? Don't your parents want you?'

No response.

That is how kids are – brutally direct. But it fucked my head up proper, because I was way too young to have the tools to deal with my family situation or even to fully understand what it meant for me. I ended up going to three local primary schools and each time my attendance was fairly poor. And yet it was still only truancy that was the problem. When I did turn up I was a good student and when it came to my final SATs I did particularly well. I was asked if I wanted to sit the exam for St Paul's with the aim of getting a scholarship to the prestigious private school. But I didn't go for it – the name meant only the cathedral to me and in any case it sounded like a poncey school that I wouldn't like. Thinking back now, I wonder how my life could have turned out differently. Perhaps I might have ended up as a lawyer or barrister as I'd always loved humanities – I was great in debates, good in conversation and I had an amazing skill in mental arithmetic, which was what led to me being given the option to sit the entrance exam. Or maybe if I'd gone to a posh school I would have just ended up doing coke instead of smoking weed...

My own secondary school of choice would have been Stoke Newington. I knew kids who were going there but my nan sent me to Gladesmore because she thought it was a better school. I was still very erratic in attending and I don't know if it would have made any difference to go to my preferred school, to be honest.

I remember Gladesmore's science building most clearly. It was a newly-built, futuristic block and it was clad in this plastic that made a shrieking noise when anyone ran their fingers along it and it got me every time. It just made me invert; it was horrible. My friend Ashley Rowe – who would later help with the video for 'Jungle' – was already at the school. He was three years older than me and a talented artist. At primary school

Ashley had drawn an amazing picture of my favourite teacher, Mrs Lysight, capturing her with her hair in a bun and a pencil in it as she always wore it. When I arrived at Gladesmore he looked out for me and said to the teacher, 'Watch this one, he's smart.' And I did surprise everyone with my ability, but only on those few occasions when I turned up at all.

I was in the top classes and the top tutor group but even as I was doing well, an absence would begin with a day off. The anxiety was always there, unless I was distracted. There were times when it was bad and times when it was worse. I'd want to curl up into a ball and hide, the fear growing in the pit of my stomach. But as a kid, how do you communicate that? I just kept telling Nan or Nanny Edie I had a stomach ache and off to the doctors we'd go.

2. THE BLUE BLANKET

Nan did everything she could for me – for all of us – and with her love I still had a lot of amazing times. Growing up without much money and with my principal carer being my nan was not always easy but at the same time it was very far from being a miserable life. She gave me the things you can't put a price on – a home, her love and her patience – though I had definitely used up her patience by the time I was aged five or six.

Although the financial situation in our house was so often perilous, I was always dressed smartly and had nice clothes. Nan made sure of that. She bought real NafNaf tracksuits alongside less successful choices too, such as a My Little Pony jumper, a green shell suit from the market and some weird stripes-meet-colours-meets-pirate-cutlass number that was almost more of a dressing-up outfit – although this was during a trip to Disneyland Paris, so can be forgiven.

Before I was old enough to choose my own hairstyle, there were some interesting decisions made by my nan (including a side parting that would make a return – along with a quiff – later on in my music career). My aunt Karen made possible some of these dodgy choices as she was a hairdresser and for a large portion of my life used to cut my hair at home. There was a period when I was older when most people had undercuts – which I avoided – but we all started getting highlights, which meant sitting in a silly rubber hat and having hairs pulled through with this weird hooky instrument which wouldn't have looked out of place in a dentist's toolkit. I used to wince at every tug. Thankfully Karen was great at what she did, though I remember others not always being as lucky with their results – a friend named Marc Murphy once looked like he had leopard spots after having it done when his hair was too short.

Nan tried to help fill the void left in my life by my parents with presents and gifts. I always had video games consoles and things like that because my nan would over-compensate in an attempt to fill the void my parents left. She often ran herself into debt with catalogues and loan sharks, and whenever someone came round to collect money I'd be sent into another room. Nan put herself under tremendous stress for me. She bent over backwards to give me these things, even though such luxuries (or what I thought of as 'luxuries') were rarely within our reach.

There was a constant worry brought on by living outside our means and through it I learned something that would stay with me for the rest of my life – that I had to work my fucking arse off for everything I wanted. As I grew older I would find that where I was born didn't have to determine where I ended up, but at the same time I was aware that none of us are born deserving of anything. We all share certain needs when we are born, needs that should be met by our mothers and fathers but quite often aren't. Why the fuck would I expect anything to just land in my lap?

My nan always made sure we had a day at the seaside through a bus that was laid on most summers to take kids from the flats to Southend or Clacton on the coast in Essex. She also took me to places such as the Lea Valley swimming pool where there was a wave machine, to Cadbury's World in Birmingham and, really stretching herself, that trip to Disneyland Paris.

Before we left for the Disney trip, my dad came over to see me. He had split up with Joyce by now, having come home one day to find she had changed the locks, and he went on to marry Jackie, the woman who was with him that day. It was dark and late and we were walking to the house behind Jackie and Nan until they went around a corner ahead of us. He stopped me quickly and pressed £70 into my hand. 'Don't you tell Jackie I've given you that, because if she knew I'd have to give it to the other kids too,' he said, meaning his step-children.

When we got back to the flat he gave me £30 spending money in front of Jackie and Nan and told me to have a good time. I was touched at the time because I knew that money was an issue for my dad, too, even if I didn't realise the true, tragic extent until after his death. I also didn't understand then that he had made that secretive gesture because he didn't have the strength to stand up for me in front of Jackie and knew that if he was found out he'd be expected to justify his actions. I remember a later Christmas at my dad's when a similar thing happened, but the other way around. We kids had finished opening our presents to find out there was one last surprise, for his step-children.

Paul, Vikki and David, had been given bicycles. I was clearly an oversight and as things became awkward my dad stuttered, 'I wasn't sure if you'd prefer money or a bike...' I don't remember Jackie being all too concerned.

Jackie didn't stop him from seeing me and I was an usher at their wedding, but she didn't encourage him to visit regularly. Dad also didn't visit the children he had with Joyce – Jason and Gary. I can't now understand how a woman could be with a man and not encourage him to see his children or how she could have any respect for a man who didn't – especially as her previous husband left her and her children. I suppose it was just an example of how nasty, selfish and jealous she is.

My earliest exposure to music came with Nan taking me to the West End to see musicals like *Joseph and the Amazing Technicolor Dreamcoat* – though I reckon that was more about her seeing her idol Jason Donovan on stage. Otherwise musical options were limited at home. My nan, bless her soul, loved her Kylie Minogue alongside Jason – I heard a lot of Stock, Aitken and Waterman's finest when I was little. And I have to admit that the first seven-inch record I ever owned was the version of 'Itsy Bitsy Teeny Weeny Yellow Polka Dot Bikini' by Bombalurina with children's TV presenter Timmy Mallett. But as that came with my nan's money, it's fair to say that she bought it. So I think I'm safe in saying the first record I ever bought myself is the far more credible 'Bad'. I was a big, big Michael Jackson fan.

I got to experience wider musical horizons through my friends' parents. Round their houses I'd hear reggae, a bit of ragga, soul, all kinds of stuff. The 'olders' (that's how my age group referred to the previous generation) played us youngers jungle. DJ Brocky, one of the jungle pioneers, lived locally and by the time I was ten I was getting all the tapes, even though I was way too young to go out to raves. I didn't really understand genres then, so I didn't even know it was dance music. I've never been much of a dancer but I was definitely into jungle. I wasn't yet into rap in a big way, although I do remember listening to Snow in 1993. I doubt even now I have the capabilities to recite 'Informer' without sounding like my nan trying to do one of my raps.

I was a big fan of East 17 – I listened to them a lot with a mate called Shane who lived on the nearby Nelson Mandela estate. With their first album named after nearby Walthamstow, Brian, Tony, John and Terry had as massive an influence on my clothes as they did on my musical tastes. I bought baggy, corduroy bottom-and-top sets by Boxer from a shop in Mare Street and Pepe jeans in pink – salmon pink. Pockets all over them. Not my only fashion faux-pas. Another favourite track was 'Let Me Be Your Fantasy' by Baby D – that got a lot of play at Lee Valley ice rink. Then I'd go back home and Nan would still be playing Jason Donovan.

The first proper rap tune that really grabbed me was Notorious B.I.G.'s 'One More Chance' remix – the more commercial single, not the album version. As soon as I heard it, I had to find out what it was. Later, I was round at my dad's, when he was living with his friend Ken by the Wick and we were watching *Above The Rim*, the basketball movie from 1994. I remember the B-side, which was a Tupac tune called 'Pain', as well as 'Regulate' on the A-side. I wasn't generally into the West Coast sound with that high-pitched whine that's prominent in a lot of the early stuff but those two tracks I loved. Soon after, we got cable at home and I became familiar with a lot more rap through shows like the mid–1990s

Yo! MTV Raps, as well as Trevor Nelson's *The Lick*. I also started buying US rap mags like *The Source* and *XXL*.

Just as my friends introduced me to new music, some of them also had grandparents who'd come to the UK from other parts of the world and I'd get to taste food from all over. Since my nan had taught me to be polite, especially to people's parents, I'd always try it even if in reality I much preferred the tried and tested: oven chips, fish fingers, beans and the like. I used to love my nan's roast dinners too and because of that I've maintained the institution of a regular roast dinner in my house. I still enjoy eating her food but she's recently admitted I make better spuds. I fucking love a potato.

I'd often watch all sorts on TV sat with uncle Mark on the sofa; Edward Woodward in *The Equalizer*, *Quantum Leap*, *Doctor Who* and a bit of comedy in the shape of Rab C Nesbitt, Roy Chubby Brown and *Bottom*. I enjoyed the piss-taking sense of humour. George at the local shop used to let me rent whatever video I wanted. I saw far too much, much too young! But all of it provided useful sources of inspiration for my lyrics later on. And I was always playing out around the flats with my mates, causing or doing myself an absolute mischief. Our flat was on the ground floor and my mates used to knock on my window. If I hadn't been to school, my nan would come to the door and say I wasn't well so I wasn't coming out. There were times when I'd wedge my door shut and climb out through the window on the sly, but I'd generally end up coming back in through the front door so there wasn't that much point in the sneaking about, to be honest.

Gangs weren't prominent on our estates when I was growing up. I get why people feel the need to join one but I never did and neither did most of my friends. We were just that: friends.

Some have continued to be mates of mine, like Felix, who grew up on an estate just opposite mine called Wigan House. He moved to Birmingham for a time when we were teenagers, but we got closer when he returned and he would eventually end up working with me.

We got up to all the stuff that kids get up to: climbing things we shouldn't, playing run outs, water fights, collecting wood for a bonfire for weeks (only for some fucking neighbor to call the fire brigade as soon as we'd lit it); there were knock-down ginger pranks too and a failed attempt at cycling to Southend. We took the most obvious route, of course – along the hard shoulder of a busy A-road. My friend Campbell's mum thought he was round the corner. As it was, we were only about ten miles into our 40-mile adventure when the police came and got us off the road.

In my area I had something that felt like an extended family, where I got to know everyone and everyone knew me and we all looked up to the older kids as children inevitably do. For a young kid it was a very closed world: Springfield Park and Hackney Marshes, which were only just over the road, seemed huge and wild, just as the forest and the seaside, where we went on our summer trips, seemed a million miles away. I had fun learning to ride my bike outside my mum's flat in Woodford, five or six miles to the east, where she'd moved to a small three-sided block near the green, though perhaps I took that for granted as I was keener to spend any amount of time with my dad – just because there was so little of it, I'd guess.

Upstairs from me lived a little girl called Chanelle who I was friendly with. Her parents were lovely but she was never allowed to get away with anything – not like I was! She moved away when we were in our mid-teens and went into acting and rapping as Shystie and later we became friends all over again – although it took a while to realise where we'd first known each other. It was funny that we both ended up in the same business even if her route to get there involved a bit more going to school than I ever managed.

One of the ways I occupied myself when I was bunking off was working in a bootlegging tape factory. I was there quite a lot, helping out. I'd put tapes on top of a magnetic machine to erase them, then set the machine to record from the master on to the blank tapes and put them into a massive box to ship out. It's funny to think that I was involved in piracy in my formative years, because I hate it now. When I got older I sometimes worked with Uncle Paul on building sites and he remembers how useless and moany I was. I had a Saturday job, too, for a while when I was 12 or 13, at a discount shop called 'This 'n' That' where my dad worked. I wasn't regular in my attendance but it gave me a chance to see my dad at least once a week.

I rolled my first spliff when I was nine, for someone else, which was a kind of rite of passage for the smaller kids. I later used that incident as inspiration for a track I featured on by Bigz called 'Grown Man Shit': 'I'm on my grown man shit – not old man shit, but old enough to tell a younger "Roll man's spliff".' I had been that younger at one point. I was smoking weed myself by the time I was 11 and I began to chip in to buy it when I was about 13 or 14. It was more common to get Thai back then, skunk was just beginning to get popular. And because it was new people would make up all sorts of dumb stuff, like saying that the strain called 'white widow' was laced with cocaine. Even then it didn't make sense to me. Why would dealers add an expensive drug to a much cheaper one? Turns out it was just THC.

I loved dogs as a kid and – apart from an Alsatian that once escaped from the block opposite mine and barely missed tearing me to pieces as I scrambled on top of a Volvo – they loved me too. I was never allowed a dog but I would make up for it when I got older.

I did get roller-skates – it was really popular in Hackney and almost as soon as I started playing out I got a pair and taught myself how to skate. That was how I first got to hear 'One More Chance' (my introduction to my then and now still favourite rap artist – Biggie), at Roller Express up in Edmonton, where they held proper raves on Saturday nights to subsidise the kids roller-skating during the days.

In the early days a group of us skated mostly in Clapton: Chanelle, Shanice, Marc and Ricky Murphy, Campbell, Lee Karl, Lee George, Lee-soi, AP, David, two other Rickys, William (and his cousin, Danny, whose sister Gemma used to go out with Marc), Danny's other sister Jamie (who had the whole flats after her), Carl and his cousin Joseph, Pedro, Daniel and Simon who lived in Nelson Mandela, Ali Malabash and his sisters (one of who was alllllllright still), Kerry, Frankie, Junior from Springfield, Felix, Marcus, Jay and his bro Robert, Ivan (whose brother Alex, aka Cores, I'd later become friends with through our mutual love for rap), Mesut and Ibrahim. Then there were the olders we were all influenced by and looked up to: Barry and Terry Laconte, Shaun and Wayne Catlin, Mark Warren (whose dad owned the aforesaid greengrocer's that my dad worked at), James Curns, Chesty, Truan, Ashley Rowe, Glen... loads of people, some names I'm sure I've forgotten but whose faces I'd remember if I met them today.

At some point or another we were all out and about on our

skates or skateboards. In those first days it was quads (four-wheeled skates) – Roces or Bauer Turbos with the tongues bent and shaped – hockey socks, coloured cheese blocks – between the heel of the boot and the frames, trucks so loose they'd always pop out, two- or three-tone Sims wheels and never any stoppers – that's what learning how to hockey-stop was for, something that we'd try and do after we'd hurtled down Big Hill or on the way home down the hill to Finsbury Park from the half-pipes at Crouch End. Whoever was in front would be throwing bags of trash – left outside shops for collection – into the path of those behind, often causing a skater pile-up. Those weren't the only injuries. On one visit Joseph managed to break his arm and, as Campbell said, 'If his skin had broken, part of his arm would have fallen off.' Grim.

AP reminded me a while ago about a fight I had with Pedro that began with a pair of skates. Barry (the older of the three brothers) had a pair of Bauer Panthers that his brother Terry sold me and I swapped them with Pedro for something or other. The only problem was that Barry had known nothing about the sale and came looking for them as soon as he found out. Barry took them back off Pedro and Pedro then wanted back what he'd swapped me. Palaver.

Ever punched your mum in the face? It sounds like something out of an Eminem lyric but it actually happened, by complete accident, when I was on my skates. Mum was chasing me. I had probably been lippy but it was all in jest. Marc snaked me and helped my mum get me, I ended up on the floor with my mum tickling me. I fucking hate being tickled, I don't have the constitution to deal with it – I'm not built like that. I begged her to stop but she carried on while my limbs moved involuntarily and whack, my hand landed her straight in the chops. I had a mere second to get out from under her while she was in shock and I made good use of the time. Sorry, Mum, but don't ever bloody restrain and tickle me again...

Only a few of us really carried on skating for any length of time. Others moved away, some simply grew out of it and then there were those who became involved in a darker side of Clapton; it was mainly just me, Felix and Jay (and through him Thomas and Kevin) on the skates with Ivan, Lee-soi and Marcus the skateboarders.

We got into more extreme versions of the sport which led to plenty of trips outside of Clapton to skate-parks and street spots we'd find all over London. People think that kids hanging round on the street, skating, get up to no good and we did, to an extent. Groups of as many of 30 of us would meet up in the City of London to skate the ledges, rails and stairs, pissing off all the building security as we did so. We were proper little shits. We got into a few scuffles with BMXers and skateboarders and smoked a few funny cigarettes but it was kids' stuff. I didn't like fighting and I'd generally do what my nan taught me: walk away. And I've never stolen anything in my life.

During one trip down to the City when I was around twelve years old I bumped into a group of guys from Surrey – Woking, to be precise: Jules, Bradshaw, Reed, Hopkins and one guy who was even bigger and taller than I was – Lewis. Lewis became a good friend, although he didn't continue skating for too long. With hindsight, he was never really made for it – he's 6-foot 7-inches now (though he claims 6-foot 8-inches) and he was big then – and he fucked up his knee not long after. I would grow to 6-foot 3-inches and I thought I was clumsy until I met Lewis, but he makes me look like a ballet dancer. Perhaps that's why we've been mates for so long and he, along with

Felix, have been the two constants in my life, with me through thick and thin.

I started watching skate videos and the American ones all featured rock music, guitar stuff, grunge – but nobody round my flat was a grunger. The soundtracks were full of Nirvana, NoFX, Blink 182 and Skunk Anansie and at first I'd just ignore the music but eventually I got into it. There's no way my music would feature all the guitars it does if it wasn't for those videos.

I was on my skates when I experienced stranger danger. Proper stranger danger: a creepy old man with a comb-over and an anorak trying to get me and mates into his car. We were playing out in the Nelson Mandela estate just behind Northwold when the bloke pulled up, apparently in a rage, accusing us of having thrown stones at his window. He told us that we had to go with him. Everyone ran except me and my mate Simon. We had just been playing hockey in the basketball court and we weren't so quick off the mark. The bloke grabbed me and I dropped my hockey stick. I don't know what would have happened if Simon's mum hadn't appeared at that moment. One of the other kids had pressed Simon's buzzer before running off. The man repeated his story to Simon's mum and gave an address nearby – we later worked out that the house number didn't exist. But even at the time Simon's mum wasn't having any of it and he got in his car and fled.

We all got taken to the police station and were interviewed. The policeman said, 'Has this taught you anything?' And I said, 'Yeah, next time I won't drop my hockey stick.' That was perhaps my best experience with the police. They were an almost constant presence around the flats and were on first name terms with the older kids. It was all very amiable, for the most part.

Life with my nan and Edie was good. I had more awareness as I got older that there was something different about our family, something missing, but Nan and Edie put food in my mouth, gave me a roof over my head and the stability every child needs and most importantly they loved me (not that I always made that an easy thing to do). I had it easy by comparison with some. There were kids I knew whose mums were using or whose dads were alcoholics or who lost a parent while they were young. There was a lot of shit in the world that wasn't mine to deal with. And yet I spent days on the sofa looking at every 253 bus that stopped outside my living room window on Upper Clapton Road, hoping that my dad was going to be on it. I'd do it for those weeks and months when he didn't visit, crying my eyes out day after day and looking out hoping he'd get off a fucking bus, but he rarely did.

But I wouldn't simply write either of my parents off as bad people. My perspective is different now and I realise it's too easy to criticise. As an adult who wants to have children myself I do hope that I can learn from them and be a better father. But I also know that it wasn't easy for them. In the end, parents are just people too, mine as much as anyone else's. They aren't and they weren't the super-beings I believed them to be when I was a kid. All parents have their own issues.

Life continued to be pretty innocent as I moved into my teenage years, although the things I got up to with my friends were the sort of larks that mark the passage of kids everywhere into adulthood. Case in point: some of my earliest tangles with the opposite sex. On a trip with everyone from the flats to Dreamland in Margate we went on a rollercoaster. My head was forced forward as we went upside down and round the loop-the-loop and I head-butted a girl called Kirsty as we completed the

nd my head came flying back. I hit another crush in the
with a ball when playing rounders at school. She pitched it,
I gave it a whack and smacked it straight in her face.

There were also the late nights in the swing park – lots of
drinking three-litre bottles of White Lightning or Hooch, going
four ways on a tens and smoking – sometimes being sick – and
going to the park or to the marshes at night with our girls to sit
on the bench and 'watch the trains go past', or to climb a tree
and smoke a spliff (great idea until you had to get down).

Then came the day I saw blood on Edie's slipper. The doctor
visited to check her over. When she got worse and the doctor
came back they called an ambulance to take her to hospital.
She wasn't a big person, Nanny Edie, but she was tough and
she hadn't been feeling unwell at all. Or if she had been, it
wouldn't have been her way to have told us. She wasn't the
sort to complain and she never liked a fuss; if she was in pain
she didn't show it. There were rare moments when you'd catch
her unawares and you could see something was wrong but not
then. I went with her in the ambulance and held her hand and
kept saying, 'You're gonna be all right. You're gonna be all
right.' And I remember her saying, 'I can't fight forever.'

To me, that was when she let go.

Once we got to hospital I tried to make her comfortable
and do things for her as she lay in bed, but she told me to stop
fussing. So I said 'Goodbye,' and left. She had a heart attack
while she was in the hospital that same night. She went into a
coma and never woke up.

My nan was planning to stay in an armchair in the hospital
overnight and I was taken to stay with my mum in Woodford.
I woke up when it was still dark, lying on the sofa, to see Mum
on the phone. She must have only just picked it up because she

hadn't even started crying, but I knew straight away what a call in the middle of the night meant. Edie had survived two world wars and two strokes and lived for years with diabetes and arthritis which must have taken some real fucking strength. Now she had finally passed on. I went straight to the hospital to be with Nan but I didn't see Edie. Later, at the funeral director's, I tried to say one last goodbye but when I saw her body I just ran out crying. I couldn't do it.

Back home after the hospital, the flat felt empty. Everything was in place, exactly how we'd left it but the fact that Nanny Edie wasn't coming back changed the way the place felt. I remembered her smile and I remembered the way she'd always fight my corner and how, sometimes, she'd argue with my nan so badly that she'd just get up and leave. Since she couldn't walk very well I'd have to run after her down the High Road to make sure she was okay and I'd always persuade her to come back. That strength was gone from my life forever.

On the day of the funeral my dad came over and we had a moment outside the flat where I'd been skating to distract myself. I can't remember everything he said but I know that I appreciated it. I guess for once he was doing what a father should and I was glad he was there for me that day.

Then it was over and Edie was gone. Nan got rid of all her things very quickly. I guess that helped her cope with losing her mum but I didn't know how to cope with the grieving and I missed having Edie's things around, all those reminders of her. It felt to my 13-year-old self like Nan was trying to pretend Edie hadn't been there at all. The thing that was most evocative and important for me – Nanny Edie's blue blanket – my nan doesn't remember at all. Recently I told her that I had been thinking of calling my fourth album

The Blue Blanket and she claimed she'd never seen it. My uncle Mark backed me up when I said I had it engraved in my memory as a feature of childhood.

Edie's passing hit me hard. Perhaps it was selfish to want her to stay with me when she had been suffering and was now at rest, but I loved her as much as I've loved anyone in the world and she was one constant element through all the turbulence of my early life. I'd never lost anyone prior to Edie. That was my first personal encounter with death. It made me feel even more forcefully that everything in my life was temporary and it became difficult to live in the moment without thinking about her having gone. Those feelings about death affected all the decisions I made: even the positive ones, the ones that resulted in me consciously choosing not to listen to my fears and anxieties, were marked by it. Thoughts of death were an unseen, negative force that dragged me down.

Edie's death took place at a delicate time in my development. Thirteen is an age at which it's natural for kids to start to push the boundaries and become more independent, and I felt like I'd lost one of my moorings. My anxiety grew worse so given the chance I increasingly stayed at home until, the year following Edie's death, I stopped going to school altogether.

3. HAUNTED HOUSE

My love for rap grew and grew into my teens. I'd religiously record the Tim Westwood rap show every Friday night on BBC Radio 1, way before DAB and streaming existed when there was such thing as a watershed and Tim and his guests on the show could speak, rap, smoke and drink freely.

I used to save up any money I earned or was given and buy tapes and CDs from Wired for Sound in Mare Street. I remember getting the LL Cool J single 'Father' just for the B-side '4, 3, 2, 1' featuring Redman, Method Man, Canibus and DMX – there was something about buying a tape having never heard it and the excitement all the way home waiting in anticipation to hear it. A lot of my memories relate to what I was listening to at the time. I remember Markey (Marcus), Felix and me all stoned listening to *Stillmatic* and in particular playing track five on repeat: 'You're da Man'. Or getting back to the flat in Hackney with Felix and Markey and playing Mobb Deep's *Murda Muzik* so loud it made my door rattle. It wasn't long before Nan came and pissed on our parade.

I bought CD versions of Canibus's 'Second Round K.O.' and a DMX album when I was 14 during my first trip to the USA. That holiday came about after Nan took me to skate at a new half-pipe in Hackney Wick and I met a couple of kids called Jordan and Blake. They introduced me to Matt King, the guy who ran the Skaters' Paradise shop in Leyton and we became mates. Matt came with me to the USA and Nan got the money together for me to travel. When I say she paid for it, what I mean is that she beyond over-stretched herself and, without me knowing, got herself in more debt. Camp Woodward ran sports-related activity weeks over the summer and was also a gymnast camp with a hot tub, so that was educational. I remember the smell of the melting tarmac beneath a blazing sun and temperatures I'd never experienced. I braved the heat to go out on my blades to buy those CDs.

My interest in rap marked me out from almost everyone else who would go on to make it big in the 2000s. Most of them started off in garage and, later, grime but I was still not into dance music despite the growing garage scene. The only English rappers I was really aware of were Roots Manuva and Iceberg Slimm and the prominent urban artists – I don't even think the word 'urban' was used in music then – were all from the garage scene. No one can deny the doors So Solid opened, along with Pay as U Go Cartel and Heartless. Wiley and Mighty Mo were my favourites back then, though the production on

So Solid's 'Rap dis' always stuck out. After that came Dizzee and a new breed of artist...

I was into the lyrical side of things. It was hip-hop that clicked with me. I love storytelling – it probably goes right back to all that time with Nanny Edie under the blue blanket – and that's what I took from rap. Some garage MCs did focus on the words but more often it was about vibes. Beats played a part for me, of course, but as I listened to every tape and CD front to back, I learned every word of pretty much every song. I'd study the tone and the delivery and the way people twisted words and made them rhyme and I loved the way rappers emphasised certain phrases. I loved the punchlines and the references you'd miss first time around and sometimes only hear years later.

I didn't know exactly the context of their everyday life in the USA but when I heard them rap, the words bridged the thousands of miles that separated us. Even though US rappers had it worse, they were describing similar shit to what I was seeing with my own eyes. There was bravado and there was exaggerating but people had nothing and were selling drugs and running guns – they witnessed with their own eyes death and poverty. It was organic, it wasn't contrived. People were documenting what was going on around them – what they themselves were living.

Biggie was the MC who really got me hooked on rap. He was charismatic; he put a piece of him in everything he did. He never sounded like he was trying: everything he did sounded effortless; the punchlines, the flow, his storytelling, nothing sounded forced. All he had to do was say 'Uh' and he'd already made his mark on a song. As cocky as he was, he was also self-deprecating and funny.

For a long time UK rappers felt they had to put on a US

accent, which might be one of the reasons it took hip-hop longer to connect with UK audiences. Skinnyman is one of the dons of the UK scene and he rapped using the same words as I did and with the same accent. Ben Hughes (12 Milagram) introduced me to Skinny, Task Force, Skinny's crew Mud Fam and others that I couldn't believe I hadn't heard of before. Ask anyone who knows about them or about Rodney P and the London Posse, Blak Twang – these guys were the pioneers of British rap. These rappers talked about places I knew and things I'd seen but still managed to rap bars that stood up to what was coming out of the USA. I'm still a fan. Once downloading became common with the likes of Napster I got hold of as much of their stuff as I could – I wasn't yet familiar with record shops that really stocked UK hip-hop and there was no such thing as iTunes back then.

For the most part it was Ivan's brother Alex and I who would really geek out over rap. I remember us walking to Wired for Sound once, why, I'm not sure – maybe because we only had the money for the CD and not enough for transport – to buy the first Canibus album; we listened to that obsessively. Canibus was for the most part a battle rapper. We couldn't wait to hear the punches he dropped on the album. I used mIRC, the old text-based internet chat service, to get music online and I remember when samples from the 2000 Eminem album, *The Marshall Mathers LP*, leaked. These were just 30 second snippets but I called Alex and everyone on a hype and told them to come and listen to them – which everyone did in a rush.

It was that shared love of rap that was the centre of a relationship that would end up with Alex and I making music together for years, Alex often working under the name Cores.

Sadly, over the years Cores and I would grow apart, to the point that we now no longer speak. But from these beginnings as kids in Hackney until just after finishing my third album, Alex would be a producer on my records, engineer most of my recordings and executive-produce every project. To not have him around now is weird, but I guess it's as simple as some people you grow with, some people you grow without.

I was quite a computer nerd when I was a kid. Markey or Minesh would come with me to the computer fair in Stratford to buy components to stick in computers and to drag back heavy monitors, normally on the S2 bus. I was inquisitive about all things technical and that's something I've lost as I've got older. Now I really don't give a toss about how anything works. I have a tiny brain and there just isn't the room for both the words and for knowing which frequencies of my voice are most annoying – the words are far more important. Markey has recently started sound engineering for me and in early 2015 we spent days traipsing around the West End in London getting equipment for the new studio, which brought back some memories of the computer fair days. But for the most part, when people now get geeky about how kit works I just put my fingers in my ears – I want it to turn on and work rather than have to learn about what it does.

My education in subjects other than music and computing was not nearly so complete given all the time I'd spent off school. My attendance got so bad that the school authorities took me out of Gladesmore. I started to attend Daniel House Pupil Referral Unit in Stoke Newington, a specialist institution designed for kids like me who, for whatever reason, couldn't stay in mainstream schools.

It was harder to bunk off from Daniel House mainly because

35

my mate Joe Dawson's mum worked there. When I took the day off school by saying I was too ill I'd sometimes see her later on at Joe's when she got back from work. Joe and I would have been there all day, smoking weed and then frantically spraying the house and ourselves with air freshener in a panicky and vain attempt to get rid of the smell.

Although my attendance improved enough for me to move on from Daniel House, it still wasn't great. Just opposite the pupil referral unit was Stoke Newington school and that was where I made my return into mainstream schooling. I was already too late to get the grades I should have done; there wasn't enough time to complete the necessary coursework. I remember the opinion of our prospects offered by one teacher at one of the two regular schools I attended. Provoked by a boy during R.E., Mr Wood finally lost it. 'I've had enough,' he said. 'You're all fucked. All of you. You're fucked. You're all going to fail. The lot of you.' And he walked out. The class was left in tears, laughing.

I began to take my first steps in making music with a crew called Haunted House Productions. I was a bit younger than them and they were more of a unit, having been together since they were all about 12. As a friend of Ivan, I'd met, hung out with and seen them quite a lot, which was how I would happen to be with them when I first rapped a lyric (well, kind of rapped). Alex and his friend David (aka Alpha-D) were both members and they gave me my introduction. I guess I felt aware of my presence when I was around them initially: they'd all been friends for so long and, being younger and as self-conscious and shy as I was, it took me a little while to feel comfortable – something I'm sure they'd all attest to. I wasn't the coolest kid. They were mainly into garage, leaving Alex, David (Alpha), Jebba (Sugarcane) and

I as the hip-hop fans alongside Adam, Jonah D, Leon (Nastie), Felix and another kid from Northwold who I'd not known so well before, Michael (aka Chyna).

My first ever rap in front of other people was totally spontaneous. I could rap along to pretty much any CD I'd ever owned but that wasn't something I did publicly. I was with Haunted House round the house of someone whose name escapes me and the others were freestyling, each taking two bars. I hadn't intended to contribute but Alpha got stuck mid-rap and I finished off a line. I supplied the line, '...or like the book itself I'm reading it'. It was only really a half-rap as all I did was end the bar and it's strange that even now I still remember it, although I couldn't tell you the rhyme David rapped to prompt me. It had something to do with a dictionary... fuck knows.

I rapped in front of the others properly for the first time at Adam's place in Bethnal Green. He was the first of the crew to get his own flat – it would be where we'd all normally buck up and play PlayStation or whatever console, watch movies and listen to music. We'd all smoke copious amounts of green (normally supplied by yours truly) and write lyrics and rap. It was just weed and computer games till the early hours, chatting shit and writing lyrics, playing beats, and writing lyrics, writing lyrics and phoning cabs up and then throwing eggs at them when they arrived, stupid stuff.

I thought I'd get slated for rapping that night. Everyone was freestyling and I got put on the spot and I just rapped a lyric there and then. I can't remember what I came up with, just that afterwards I wanted to curl up and hide under the table. And everyone else just looked at me like, 'G'wan, you can rap, you know.' And that's where it started.

It was around the same time that I finished with my first serious girlfriend, Sarah. I always had pretty good luck with women and would normally manage to punch well above my weight. God knows how I used to do it, because for years I looked like I'd tried to eat a television, thanks to that childhood accident with the sofa. It wouldn't be until I got the deal with Virgin in 2009 that I got my teeth fixed. In hindsight it was probably the gift of the gab that helped me with women, in the same way it later on would help me with my career. That said, I grew up with two very, very strong women as role models and that gave the women in my life a lot to live up to.

For most of my life I've been a serial monogamist. My first three proper relationships each lasted around three years and I had met Sarah when I was 15 through her brother. She was there for that stoned *Stillmatic* session with Felix and Markey and it was when I was with her that I had a bout of glandular fever that landed me in hospital. I was on my third course of antibiotics when I woke Sarah one night by loudly choking in my sleep. Nan took me to A&E at the local hospital where they thought I had an abscess in my throat. Nan thought I'd been putting it on and at this news was quite apologetic, but then I had bunked off school enough times in the past. The nurse told me I should go and tell the person who gave me the glandular fever – also known as the 'kissing disease'. Sarah didn't have it, so essentially that nurse was accusing me of cheating on my girlfriend while lying in my sickbed – not exactly what I needed to hear when I was ill. Nor did I want to hear a story from my dad's wife, Jackie, who during her visit told me all about a friend of her's who nearly died from it.

Sarah was a much more successful student than me. She pretty much got straight As in her GCSEs and went on to City and Islington college in Holloway Road. I ended up leaving Stoke Newington without even turning up for my exams but I wasn't ready to give up quite yet. I followed Sarah to the college in an attempt to catch up and re-take (or rather take for the first time) some key subjects. But I didn't do any better and blew my chances without once having entered an exam hall. That was the end of my educational career.

I got taken on as an apprentice with a desktop publishing company called Select Typesetters. I'm sure I didn't look like the most promising candidate on paper what with my lack of any qualifications. But I had an introduction from my friend Michael – Chyna from Haunted House – who had put a good word in for me. He knew that I was good with computers after all those years making websites, skate videos, downloading videos and learning how to pirate Dreamcast games. I would end up staying with Select for five years, working on graphics, letterheads and logos, putting text into layouts, applying styles and I did well at it.

The company were genuinely very good to me, particularly an older guy called Colin who worked at reception and was also the proofreader. He took me under his wing, helped me along and put up with a lot from me. I was often bored by the work at Select and I used to get caught listening to music all the time. Chyna and I spent a large part of our days emailing back and forth with lyrics. Jay-Z said that when he was hustling on the corner he would make lyrics up in his head and file them away for retrieval when he had the opportunity to put them on tape. It was something I did too but there were times when I lost lyrics or only remembered that I had something worth remembering without actually remembering what it was. Jay- Z also said he didn't smoke weed.

With my schooling having gone nowhere and my work ambitions seemingly confined to learning the ropes at Select, my childhood dreams of getting a career in the law had disappeared completely. My options had become much more limited if I wanted to make more money – at least, legally. But there was one way to make some ready cash that many kids like me took. It was everywhere around me, in plain sight and it was selling weed. I didn't really even consider weed to be a drug as such and I didn't think there was anything wrong in smoking it. 'Shotting' was what we called dealing and nearly everyone did a bit on the side to subsidise what they were smoking. I started out in a casual way by selling to mates and ended up being a drug dealer. I would take shotting a lot further than most people I knew and by the time I quit I had made it into a sometimes successful business.

I began by going in with a friend on an ounce when I was around 17. We split it by estimating rather than weighing it, sold some on and didn't have to pay for what we smoked. That was all there was to it – buy a piece of weed, sell a bit among your mates and Bob's your uncle. But then it started to sell and my link – we'll call him Dave – asked if I wanted to take on a bigger bit. The idea of taking it further crossed my mind for the first time, but again only in a casual sense. I thought, Yeah, I suppose I could get rid of it. And so it went on.

I was as good at this work as I was at the legit job: I was trustworthy and any losses – there were a few – I always made back myself. I didn't deal as part of a gang or with a crew and I wasn't selling to make a reputation for myself. The opposite was true. I didn't want anyone to know what I was doing if they didn't have to. I kept myself to myself and I'd pick up larger quantities every time I'd re-up. Slowly but surely I progressed from parcelling weed out by eye to borrowing my nan's kitchen scales, then to buying some of those little black Tanitas and finally to owning a great, big set of white pans that weighed kilos at a time. I started to use cling film more often than button bags as I'm sure the local stationer shop started to be slightly suspicious about why a gangly white guy in a fitted cap and an oversized Avirex had so many buttons.

The work had some tangible benefits aside from the money. I had a lot of time to do other things, which was useful when I was working on music. And shotting could be very social; I travelled from one mate's house to another, from one sofa to the next. Roll in, roll up, have a cup of tea and listen to some music and play computer games until the next call came and I was out the door again. Days were filled with smoke, good music and chat. And money in folds of tenners – ten-folds, jibs in elastic bands. (A jib, or a quid, is £1,000 and also known as a bag of sand – a grand. We'd call £500 a monkey. There was a lot of slang. Twenty pounds is a score. When I first slapped someone over a score I realised I was beginning to change.)

For a while I moved weed on public transport but I quickly worked out that was a mug's game. I came out of a station one evening and the barriers were surrounded by police with dogs in one of their random swoops. By pure chance I wasn't carrying anything. Before then I hadn't wanted to waste money on minicabs but now they seemed like good investments. I got cabs everywhere and there was no way that the cabbies weren't wise to what I was doing. As one of them dropped me off in Camden he raised an eyebrow and said 'Something smells aiiight!' I dropped him a couple of buds as he went on his way.

I don't know how I used to do it without getting paranoid. Just thinking about some of the situations now is enough to make me feel anxious. I was often in a cab with a police car right behind and sat there with a boot full of skunk. Or the time, much later, when I was sitting on a National Express coach coming back from buying some rather special bits and bobs off a link I'd met out of town while on tour. I had decided it was better not to put it in the hold so I had the bag with me but it was winter and the coach heating was on full. The smell ripened with every passing minute and spread through the cabin. What if they'd called forward to the police and I got off at Victoria coach station and got nicked? How I had the audacity to sit there barefaced like I was doing nothing wrong is beyond me now. These days, I can't go near a skunk spliff – two draws and the paranoia creeps in. I don't touch that stuff anymore, well, not really.

As I dealt more, my runnings kept on getting bigger and so did the quantities. I'd normally walk out of the estate in Dalston with two or three old-style chequered laundry bags. I'd either have a cab waiting or take a short walk to the cab office. I'd get a mate to come and meet me near the flat when I got home. He would carry them up as though they were his so as not to raise suspicion and soon after he'd leave with the bags too – although not with their contents.

Nan initially didn't have a clue about what was going on. She had never smoked weed and she'd never been around it, so for a long time she didn't know what was happening under her nose and didn't recognise the smell that was wafting past it. But her innocence couldn't last. One day she went over to one of her friend's houses and smelled the odour familiar from home. So she asked about it and was told, 'So-and-so's smoking weed.' When she came home, she hit the fucking roof. I didn't know what to say. But I did know that I couldn't have my nan anywhere near harm's way. I didn't like the thought that I might one day bring trouble to her doorstep.

I moved out to Woodford with Nan, not long after my 18th birthday, my last in Clapton. That birthday also marked, although I had no way of knowing at the time, the last occasion on which I saw my father. For me, it was just another birthday. I did the typical kid thing and barely had any time to speak to my dad. Sarah was there and my friends too, and I was too busy having a good time to focus on him. Part of the reason we didn't see each other again was that we went through one of those all-too-familiar lengthy periods when Dad didn't get in touch with me, but there was a difference this time. I was older and sick of the disappearing act; it wouldn't be me or Nan that made the first move this time. And so it would be more than five years before I finally gave in and phoned him but by then time would have almost run out for us.

My mum had lived in the flat in Woodford prior to us. Mum wanted to move back to Hackney and it seemed like a valid way of getting Nan out of harm's way so we did a flat swap. Living in Woodford full-time, as opposed to visiting my mum, was a bit of a trip for a kid from Hackney. It's right out by Epping Forest on the north-east edges of London and it feels more like the country than the town. I remembered seeing cows grazing on the lawn outside the flats when I used to visit Mum, but by the time we moved there they had put in cattle grids and there weren't so many cows after the country-wide epidemic of foot-and- mouth earlier in 2001.

I went on dealing as before but now my home was completely separate from my business and it felt safer. It was easier to keep a low profile.

My relationship with Sarah came to an end, just before the move. Sarah and I had been arguing loads – one falling-out in particular led to a bunch of us heading from Hackney to Holloway, most of the group travelling by moped, though I took the bus along with a few others. Her phone had been answered by some dickhead who was in a drama production she was taking part in. Another man answering her phone was like a red rag to a bull and he was too mouthy at the other end of the line. We found them in a pub they'd often go to after rehearsals, The Hobgoblin on Holloway Road. I walked in on my own and with me there he was suddenly a lot more polite. He wouldn't come outside, I ended up in a blazing row with Sarah, her brother got involved and we ended up in a swingers. All pretty pointless, ego-driven and juvenile. There was some back and forth between Sarah and I for quite some time, but that was the end of the relationship.

That was just one of many moped-powered dramas, although I didn't have my own machine at that point – I did get one later but only for a tragically short time. It was my uncle Paul who lent me money to buy a moped and, as I didn't have my CBT, Felix went to pick one up for me. He got chased by the police and when we heard the sirens we pulled the bins out of the rubbish chute, Felix drove straight into the chute, jumped off the bike and we pushed the bins back inside to hide it and shut the doors. Everyone walked off and the police roared in and looked around but were none the wiser.

When they'd gone I got on the bike and decided to go for

what turned out to be a very brief ride with Ivan and Alex. We shot up to Stamford Hill and then came back to Northwold. Another friend, Kurt, wisely said, 'You've had a ride, now park it off, leave it for tonight.' A great piece of advice I obviously didn't listen to. We went down to Ivan and Alex's house then headed back to mine. I got to a right turn with a car to my left and Ivan decided to cut me up, coming between me and the car. I tried to straighten up, turned late, got thrown off the bike and hit a fucking bollard, chest first. Another kid called Rasheed had just walked out of the estate when it happened and saw the whole thing. He managed to grab my log book as it blew down the road – my seat had come off the bike in the crash and everything stored in it was emptied on to Upper Clapton High Road.

I made it back home on foot. I was just relieved that I hadn't turned as I flew through the air because if I'd hit that bollard with my back I wouldn't have bent around it so easily and there would have been a very different ending to the story. Even so, I still felt fucked and went into the bathroom where I coughed up blood into the sink. I looked into and felt the inside of my mouth but there weren't any cuts. I coughed again – more blood and I began to worry. My nan called the ambulance and at hospital they found I'd got a fracture in my shoulder and blood on my lungs. I was fucked, but at least the blood was only from the impact and I hadn't punctured a lung. I couldn't laugh without wincing for a little while after that.

Continuing to do music with Haunted House, I was rapping as Professor Green by the time I was 19, the name having come about as a product of one of the many nights at Adam's. Jonah had said something inaccurate about weed and I corrected him on it. He said, 'All right. What are you? Some kind of professor? Professor Green?' And it just stuck. Before that I had been known as OZ (pronounced 'Oh-zed') but it was a shit name and I'm glad Jonah came up with the alternative, even if I have the occasional reservation about it as I get older. Now I'm married and looking forward to having a family I think about having to explain it to my kids. ('Dad, Dad... why are you called Professor Green?') But then I think, fuck it, it's all right, my kids will be hippies who'll be smoking homegrown by the age of 12.

My first ever gig as Pro Green was on a stage set up just outside Hackney town hall at a showcase for local talent during a community fun day and show. Haunted House were one of the bigger attractions and we were on the bill quite late. I had to spit my lyric on a Haunted House track called 'Football'. Felix had a verse on it too and Lewis, who I'd met when we were kids while skating, was there. He's probably still got a recording of it on a hard disk somewhere. I was wearing my baby-blue Avirex and a fresh pair of Nike Air Max Ltds with Professor Green sprayed in graffiti letters on the outside and Dexter from *Dexter's Lab* and Alvin, Simon and Theodore, the fucking Chipmunks, sprayed on the inside. I'd got them from a shop in Bethnal Green – Meteor Sports – where everyone used to go.

Garage was making the shift to grime roughly around this time – I forget when, exactly, but for me grime came into prominence through Wiley from Pay As U Go, Dizzee, Kano, D Double E, Demon, Bruza, Titch, Ghetts and the like.

All the elements of my life were then happening in parallel. I did a bit of everything – listening to a lot of music, doing my own thing with Haunted House, working a nine-to-five job and shotting. In fact while I was up there on stage at Hackney town hall there was a car parked down the road with kilos of food in the boot.

At Select I'd rather do anything other than what was in my inbox, so I'd always be the one to volunteer to get everyone's lunch, on the basis that 20 minutes standing in a queue in a sandwich place was better than sitting at my desk – and if I had stuff to drop off and queues were big I could stretch it out to almost an hour of freedom.

It was on one of those midday excursions that I saw a poster for a hip-hop night called Lyric Pad, at Oh Bar in Camden, which hosted rap battles every month. I went back to the office, told Chyna and later that week we went down for the first time.

Battle rapping was stressful, but I always was a glutton for punishment and, as Lewis always tells me when I'm whining about things fucking up, I work better under pressure. The whole point was to come up with the wittiest, nastiest, personal and relevant rhymes about the opponent, saying them to his face as he stood there waiting to retort. There was never any predicting the outcome. I had to stand there and try to slow my racing thoughts enough to structure rhymes in my head – all the while pretending not to be paying the competition any attention, but listening to every word, hoping something would spark an idea for a reply. Pre-written rhymes weren't accepted back then, so taking what your opponent said and flipping his or her bars in your own was a great way to prove you were freestyling. I won my first battle that night but I don't remember much about it. Like the gigs with Haunted House, this wasn't a defining moment at the time – it wasn't as if I got a sense that this was what I was going to be doing for the rest of my life. It was much more spontaneous as that was just the nature of these events. It was a matter of being in these situations as they happened. You had to be there...

I can't explain how I took to it. As a child I had been shy and chubby , and didn't show any kind of signs of taking this kind of thing on while growing up. It had taken me just over a year or so to get myself to the point where I would stand on a stage in front of a room full of people who wanted to see me fuck up, having to face competitors I didn't know who were ready to cuss me, my clothes, my family, anything they thought was a weakness. But the buzz I got from it brought me right back the next month. It was at this next battle that I first met Skinnyman. As I arrived I recognised him immediately, having a smoke outside and I thought, shit, he's gonna battle.

So I rang Chyna who said, 'What are you gonna do if he does?'

I answered, 'Battle him, innit!' But that could have ended badly: Skinny isn't one to run out of bars. As it turned out, Skinny didn't compete and I lost the battle, but it wasn't a disaster and I began what would be a lasting friendship with Skinny. He was really good to me in those early days as I was just starting to find my way.

That same night I heard about the Jump Off, a regular MC battle run by two brothers, Harry and Ara, and in November 2003 I took part in the Jump Off for the first time, when it was at the tail end of being held at Sound nightclub in Leicester Square, just before it moved to The Scala in King's Cross. I followed it to the new venue.

Jump Off was intensely competitive. People converged from all over with their mates and their crews. I was among wolves. There were huge sections of the crowd that didn't want anyone to win: they wanted everyone to fuck up. I mean, the better I did, the more they'd get behind me but if I slipped up they were unforgiving. There was no point at which they liked battlers enough not to tear them apart for one shit rhyme, one choke.

I lost that first battle at Jump Off – to a guy called Roky – and I knew there and then that I wasn't gonna have that again. I beat him the following three times we battled and I enjoyed every single one of those wins.

I've only got a couple of pictures of my mum, dad and me together. Here's one of them, just after I was born in 1983 (*top*) – as well as an early picture of me and my aunt (*above left*) and me showing an early interest in vinyl a few years later (*right*).

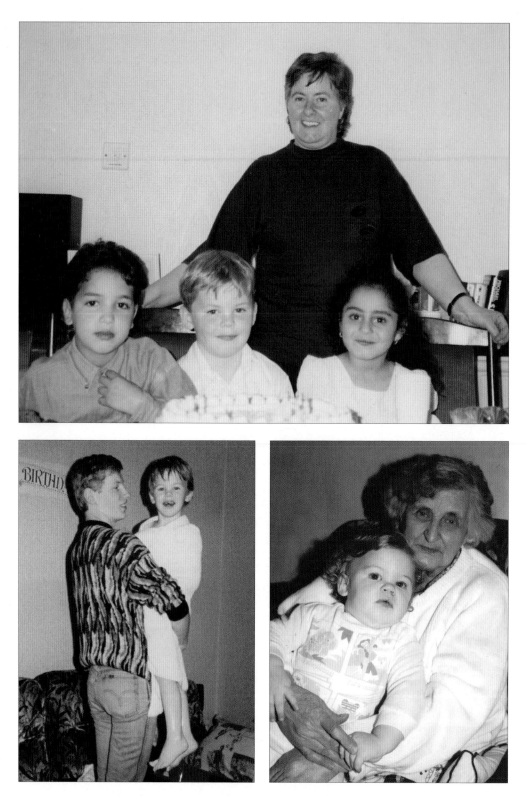

My nan, Patricia (*top*), and my nan's mother Edie (*above right*) brought me up, initially on the Northwold Estate in Hackney. My dad was an occasional presence in my life, but as you can see I was always happy to see him (*above left*).

At school, for once, sporting an early version of my side parting (*top*). Then there's me and a pal, Lee. He dressed sensibly in an Arsenal jersey – and me with highlights in my hair and a NafNaf jumper. Forgive me.

Here's one of my early birthday parties at the hall in the middle of my old estate, Northwold (*above*). Truan, me, Ali Malabash and Karim, all smiling. Then there's one with Marc Murphy in the distance, taken on a trip to Crystal Palace just after I made the transition from quad-skates to blades.

I was hanging out with celebs from a very early age. Here's me with my nan's hero Jason Donovan (well, a superimposed Jason Donovan!). And one with a top-side soul grind, on a red rail we actually got welded ourselves in Wrens Park.

Here I am looking confused – probably as to why I'm wearing these silly headphones during my first proper video shoot for the remix of The Streets' 'When you wasn't famous'. Note the aptly placed *Heat* magazine nearly falling out of my tracksuit bottoms, which are nearly falling off me!

New Era caps, Avirex jackets, Iceberg History, long-sleeves with Snoopy on. . . Also a lot less hair than I have now. I think these two were from my first press-shoot, just before my eyes started to stream due to the equivalent of snow blindness caused by the ring flash! ©Cary Hammond

©Alex Koo

©Paul Hampartsoumian

Here I am having become the first person to win the Jump Off seven times in a row (*top*), following up with a second set of seven wins not even a year later (*bottom*).

4. THE JUMP OFF

I'd made a name for myself through battling and, for the most part, winning at Jump Off when I heard that Mike Skinner wanted to meet with me. The Streets had broken through to the mainstream and he was getting to the height of his success. I hadn't really paid The Streets much attention and, if I thought anything, it was that he wasn't a great rapper. At work we were only allowed to listen to BBC Radio 2, so at least hearing 'Dry Your Eyes' when it got to UK No 1 in the summer of 2004 made the day at Select marginally more interesting by being one of the few rap tracks the station played. I just didn't quite realise exactly just how important his music was at the time.

I had moved out from Nan's and now shared a two-bedroom flat in Holloway, north London with my girlfriend Naoko. Holloway was more central and put me in the mix of things;

it was easier to go out at the drop of a hat without the daunting journey back to Woodford. It meant I still had a chance of getting a brief bit of kip after a night out before it was back to reality at Select Typesetters. I saw a lot of Skinny and some of his pals as well – Fatboy and Afro (who you can hear mentioned in the freestyle on my first mixtape, when Skinny brought me out on stage at Islington Academy), Moesy and his brother Michael and Nasar.

I was never really into going to clubs or drinking (how that changed) but I now began to frequent a lot of the regular nights. Along with Haunted House Productions, I'd sometimes go to Sports Bar in Wood Green or a pub in Stokey (Stoke Newington), but for the most part we'd just jam at someone's house or in the flats – if not going out on the High Road shouting 'Oi' at girls we tried to draw down... There were nights at Herbal and Ministry, open mic nights at Deal Real Records and Kung Fu at the Underworld in Camden – places where Skinny knew everyone and we rarely had more than a minute's wait at the door.

These were pre-smoking ban days and you could bun a spliff in a dance – although not always without hassle. I remember one new year security gave one of us shit about smoking a spliff. Yet the smell of fucking coke spliffs was far stronger than our skunk.

My relationship with Naoko lasted for quite a while, despite what was a shaky first date: we went to a night that started at Deal Real Records, freestyling and hanging out. I was walking down a dingy alley in Soho with Leon Humphries, a mate from my skating days, to meet Naoko, when a patrol car showed up behind. I had a few shots in a little bag (tucked between my right bollock and thigh inside my boxers. I always favoured the right bollock; it hangs lower). I quickly turned the next corner, pulled the bag out, ran and dropped all the shots over a railing by some stairs. Slowing down to a less suspicious pace I carried on walking to meet Naoko. After a quick hello and a kiss on the cheek, our night began with me saying, 'Listen, I need to go round the corner and pick something up round there...'

Naoko was half-Italian, half-Japanese and shared my passion for music. She liked many of the same artists too – even today she pesters me to hear my new lyrics when we hang out. Through Naoko my horizons were broadened in many ways. She is an amazing cook and her adventurous food was a revelation for someone like me who had grown up on traditional English fare. I learned how to cook for myself – although the lessons were not always pain-free. Once she had me chop chillies and I only washed my hands before I chopped them rather than afterwards. I went to the toilet where an interesting, tingling sensation quickly boiled over into an overwhelming heat. With my trousers round my ankles, I ended up lying on the bed asking – begging – for a cold flannel. She somehow found one between bursts of highly sympathetic laughter.

It wasn't just new cuisine Naoko introduced me to. After an initial argument when I found out she'd taken MDMA on a night out (I had learned to sell things rather than take them) I eventually took my first pill with her and Kemi at our house. I was completely unimpressed and sat on a sofa smoking a spliff, saying that I didn't see the attraction and that it wasn't doing anything. Naoko and Kemi started laughing and asked me what I was doing fidgeting and rubbing my thighs...

Through Naoko I met a bloke called Luke – I think it was at a birthday party for Naoko at the flat. Luke and I discovered we had similar tastes in music and it turned out that when he was younger he had also been involved in knocking bits out. He and Naoko went to the same college and had been pally for years. It was in bed that night that I mentioned how cool Luke was, to which Naoko said, 'You know he's gay, right?' Now, I'm not sure I was ever really homophobic but there were some pretty harsh views on being gay where I grew up and I guess I kind of took them on board as my own, though I'd never been hateful to anyone who was. But I – we all – threw the term around as an insult. Anyway, I thought she was having me on as he wasn't in the least bit camp and my idea of someone who was gay was the stereotypical flamboyant and camp male who spoke a little bit like Loyd Grossman. He was none of these things. I didn't believe Naoko so she said, 'Phone him.' I did. Yep. Gay. Slightly awkward phone conversation, but from that day on I've been exempt of any prejudice I ever had and slightly embarrassed that there ever had been any.

That said, we all went out for one of Luke's birthdays to a bar in King's Cross. Everyone was going on to a gay night at the Coronet in Elephant and Castle and they convinced me to tag along. Naoko was there so I figured I'd hold on to her for dear life. Having spent a large part of the evening with one of Luke's mates who looked like TV presenter Andi Peters telling me how many straight guys he'd turned I didn't think it could get much worse, so I went along. I was wrong. Luke almost punched someone who grabbed my arse and going to the toilets was one of the scariest things I've ever witnessed. Scarred for life, though mentally, not anally.

Things were pretty steady for a while; I plodded along at Select, there was a buzz building around my name in music and there were no dramas with shotting – I was as financially comfortable as I'd ever been (which was not very). I wasn't primarily into it for the money side of things, but my 'tick list', or accounts, began to contain larger numbers. I didn't drive, so I didn't splash out on cars. I just spent a lot living well, going out with my mates and I also bought a lot of clothes. Lewis says now that my clothes buying was out of control: I certainly owned a lot of Nike trainers and Avirex jackets. I'd usually take a trip up west on the weekend to grab something new to wear on the Monday at Jump Off. Most of my clothes were never bought in sizes that actually fitted – we all had oversized outfits, huge tracksuits always on the verge of falling down (I'm not quite sure what the whole XXL phase was about). I bought Iceberg History from Le Homme in Soho, Probito and House of Labels as well. The Akademics tracksuits and Avirex jackets I'd buy from Mods on Oxford Street. A large part of my prized collection was later binned by total accident. I had left them at my mum's after moving out and the box got thrown out with its Sylvester and Tweetie Pie t-shirts and Donald Duck denim jackets and jeans.

Disposable income was one of the few benefits of the life of a dealer, but I couldn't say it was a glamorous existence and there were frequent hassles. I'd get wet food that would sweat and rot and be useless. Or there'd be spider mite, which was the worst. I can't count the fucking hours I spent trying to pick shit out of near-ruined skunk, cutting portions into ever smaller bits and trying to make it look presentable. There were times when I'd be stuck with dead, dead, *dead* food, thinking, How the fuck am I ever gonna get rid of this? I'd have to get more food and mix the bad in with the good.

On a more serious level, there were near misses with the law and encounters with jackers – people who didn't have the heart for the graft and took rather than made. Other dealers I knew got caught and were put inside. I was in Haggerston once, walking out of a flat with two laundry bags and in the middle of the narrow street was a police car that had pulled someone over. Panic. 'Keep walking,' I told myself, 'you'll be fine. You're just a guy in baggy jeans and a fitted cap carrying grandma's laundry bags and they're far too busy dealing with the blokes they've already tugged. What's there to worry about?' Then I turned left and there were two uniformed officers walking towards me. And the bags stunk. They reeked. But the police walked straight past and I managed to get to the cab office.

My luck threatened to run out on me on one or two occasions, not least on the day a few friends got turned over by jackers – right in the middle of a drought just as some bloody food had landed. We were sitting in the living room, everything was cool until the front door caved in and the flat was suddenly full of people. The next thing I knew my friend was in the doorway with a knife held to his throat. There were more of them than us, all ballied up and we had no means of protection; it wasn't the most pleasant of situations. Needless to say I lost a few quid.

But the experience didn't give me second thoughts about dealing. I was in it and that was just the way it was. It wasn't my beef, it wasn't my house; I just happened to be there. I went to see my link, Dave, to explain there was gonna be a delay on what I owed him and to see if I could grab something to start working off the debt... In other words, I just got on with it. I linked up with a pal in Stoke Newington and came back later to where the drama had happened. We had a spliff and went over the events of the day. But this time there was a strap on the table – just in case.

By this point people were starting to catch wind of what I was doing – I was probably better known locally for that than I was for the music. It made things hotter for me and, to top it off, a hostel – the type people go into when they're on their way to getting a council flat – was opened right next door to where we rented our flat. You could almost climb over to mine from their roof terrace. Not ideal: I couldn't even smoke a spliff on my balcony, let alone be sure all my comings and goings weren't being watched. But I had to make back the money from the stolen food and I did.

Jump Off was getting bigger and so was I, becoming the first competitor to win seven weeks in a row, often in the company of Haunted House and Skinny. I was briefly banned from The Scala in a personal dispute with the manager, but he left the venue and Jump Off wanted me back. So I got back into it, got the itch and ended up winning seven weeks in a row all over again. I competed in the final in August 2004 and with that victory I became Jump Off's first MC champion. The pressure was always high but I thrived on it.

Skinny always said that freestyling was dangerous – you draw from your unconscious so at any given moment truths are liable to come flying out. I never quite knew where the rhymes were going to lead me and I would often end up getting into whatever was on my mind mid-cipher. With battling I was more focused. My approach was to pace before I got on stage, talk to people, do anything I could to take my mind off the battle to come and stop myself from overthinking. The less I had cluttering up my tiny brain the better.

When I was up there I'd stand with my back to the other rapper, giving them absolutely nothing, no sign I was even listening – if I rose to the bait I'd be validating what the person was saying and that would give the crowd a reason to get behind my opponent. And yet my mind would be racing, working out comebacks to lines I'd just heard, even if I wasn't quite sure how I'd make them rhyme. When the mic was handed to me I drew in the audience by occasionally talking about the other rapper as 'him' rather than 'you', making my approach more conversational and helping to engage the audience. The audience would dictate the vibe of the battle: a backpack crowd would follow the complexity of multis and metaphors and would get the rap references, while a commercial crowd preferred things to be dumbed down. Humour could be a powerful tool.

I remember one Jump Off to which I returned as the previous week's winner. I was watching the new competitors battle before I took on whoever got to the final when I saw a battler who looked a lot like the Milky Bar Kid – to me, at least. It was pretty obvious from his first battle it was likely to be him I'd meet in the final and I prayed no one else noticed and used the reference. They didn't and after I compared him to an overgrown sperm, Mini-Me from *Austin Powers* and then the Milky Bar Kid, the whole room fell about screaming with laughter. That was one of those moments of magic when the words took me somewhere almost before I realised what was happening. It all came together – click, rhyme – and I came out with something I'd barely even knew I'd thought.

I recorded my own four-track sampler, the first thing I ever produced of my own for public consumption. I did it with Cores – my friend Alex – pressed up some CDs and I gave it out at every opportunity – when I was at the Jump Off, at the Lyric Pad and everywhere else I went. Haunted House Productions went on to land a regular slot on Kiss FM. The station had run a competition to host a show with the winner being decided by the public. Haunted House got the prize after we printed up CD samplers and went up to the West End and hustled, convincing listeners to vote for us. All the years listening to and appearing on pirate radio had paid off.

My vocals then sounded much as they do today; the flow and the tone have been fairly consistent from the start. But I found it hard to get used to hearing my voice back. Since those first attempts at putting tracks down I have used my voice in so many different ways but, ultimately, whenever I put energy into what I do, I end up sounding like a 12-year-old. Over the years I've learned to deal with that although I've never got over my dislike of hearing recordings of myself talk. It's acutely embarrassing even now and the reason I tend not to watch or listen back to anything I've done apart from songs and music videos.

I saw a lot of Skinnyman. He drew a lot out of me in those early days which definitely gave me more confidence in what I was doing. Skinny always had a vibe and always had a lyric. He'd often drive to wherever we were going, unless we jumped in a cab or hopped on a bus, often freestyling all the way there, us both going back and forth. At Dingwall's in Camden, Skinny brought me out on stage with other rappers including Farma, Chester and a few others. It was kinda mad for me to think I had only been introduced to their music a couple of years earlier and now I was on stage with them all. I'm still a fan of Skinny's 2004 album, *Council Estate of Mind*; for me it will always be the best album to come out of the UK. The two of us recorded a song together at the same Camden studio where he'd done most of the album but the hard drive went bang and we never even heard it back.

Friday night normally meant the open mic sessions at Deal Real Records. I can't emphasise the vibe enough, how important Deal Real was for the scene. The place was never edgy and didn't have the tension you'd find elsewhere. There were always UK artists in attendance, American artists passing by the store if they were in town and spontaneous battles. It's a shame all of that has gone now they've closed down, though they did have a pop-up in 2015 – who knows, maybe Deal Real will open permanently again. I remember that during ciphers there, I used to read the names on the vinyl on the shelves and use them in my raps. An undercover cop once noticed Skinny with a spliff (along with everyone else who was there). He began to introduce himself as a copper and Skinny didn't look at all bothered. The officer went on to say he was going to need to search him. 'Okay,' said Skinny, pausing for comic effect before pushing him out of the way and running for it.

On the blocks, whether with other rappers or not, I'd always be rapping shit amongst my friends. At the Jump Off or at Lyric Pad I'd annoy the hell out of Lewis by standing behind him, freestyling in his ear. As the battle progressed in front of us I would rap bars about both the guys on stage from my vantage point in the crowd. Lewis would complain, 'Chill the fuck out, bro!' I was probably interrupting valuable drinking time or something.

When I wasn't rapping I was writing lyrics. Freestyles didn't get committed to paper but when inspiration struck elsewhere I looked to record it. If I couldn't tape what I was thinking I scribbled down words, filling pads, writing emails and saving my thoughts via instant messaging. These were the most convenient ways of keeping hold of my ideas, given that I'd still usually be writing when I was stuck at Select, in a cab or on sat on someone's sofa.

I was making my name quickly. The UK rap scene was small and the community was tight. There weren't really the equivalent hip-hop club nights of garage's Twice As Nice or Pure Silk. The hip-hop nights in London tended to cross over into R&B and would generally only play US rap. Homegrown rapping talent was underground and grimy and that was reflected in the clubs. You wouldn't have come to Kung-Fu for the glamour or chicks. Jump Off was best at bridging the gap between a West End club night while retaining its edge. The size of the scene meant that Jump Off was not only a good training ground but a great place to meet people. Almost all my pals in rap and the people I worked with in my early years I got to know through Jump Off and, if not there, then through Skinny – he knew just about everyone. He didn't only introduce me to people, he also introduced me to the lethal combination of champagne and Red Bull.

I had started to see a music industry guy called Tim Medcraft around, who worked in music publishing and after a while he said he was interested in working with me. I wasn't good at getting back to him and it wasn't until we met later at a music conference in Manchester, where Jump Off hosted a battle, that Tim gave me his card. He came from a publishers called Bucks. We worked together for more than seven years, although it got off to a rocky start. After a couple of emails I'd missed he sent one last one to say that he was serious. Did I want to do this? So I had a meeting with him – at the pub next to the Bucks offices in west London. It was the first step to me signing for them for what was barely any money although he'd later say he'd taken a real risk signing me. But it was a start, though even then I looked at it as a stepping stone. Tim wasn't risking a great deal with the size of the advance but I think it's fair to say that he took a punt considering there hadn't been many commercial UK hip-hop successes and I hadn't written many songs at that time.

It was a period of unlimited and constant creativity for me. I met new people all the time. Those long, smoky evenings messing around at Adam's with the whole crew happened all the time – I took it for granted when I now have to make an appointment for everything and squash my studio time around meetings, promotion, interviews, conference calls and a million other things.

I was learning my craft, working out the different skills needed to hold a stage by battling and by performing with a crew. It took me a while to get my head round it. I didn't understand how to project my voice at gigs, and while I was always good with a crowd, it took me a while to develop the vocal stamina needed to play a full set of songs, not to mention to write enough songs for a solo set.

I supported myself largely by dealing. Music and shotting were the biggest parts of my life and were more exciting than the day job. I had enough coming in to cut my working days at Select down to three from five.

When I got the word that Mike Skinner wanted to meet me, it came after he had seen me rap at Brixton Academy, at the B-Boy Championships, where Jump Off had been hosting rap battles between the rounds. He was then living just down the road in Streatham. I didn't know what Mike had in mind for me and I hadn't been that interested in The Streets before so I went back to listen to his albums and I realised I had missed something. This time I was blown away. Before now I hadn't understood what he was doing. I was so immersed in hip-hop that I expected everyone who rapped to rap a certain way while he brought something very different to the table. He took in everything around him and he had given it a British spin on 2002's *Original Pirate Material* in a way that few albums across any genres have managed. He defined the sound of a generation, taking influences from so many places. I later found out that he did his own production and when I got to know him better I learned that he obsessed over everything until it sounded just as he wanted. He had made one of the most important and influential albums of the last 20 years.

I was excited and a bit intimidated about meeting him, particularly as he sent a car to Select to take me to a restaurant for lunch. I was pretty used to cabbing round when I was shotting but at this point I don't think I knew anyone with an Addison Lee cab account. I was wearing a light-blue Stone Island top and a pair of Evisus and the driver looked at me doubtfully. He suggested that perhaps I'd got in the wrong car. I thought for a moment I'd got the dress code wrong but it turned out the driver assumed he was picking up a professor of the grey-haired, academic kind.

The restaurant was on the banks of the Thames by Tower Bridge and was a French place with wine bottle-lined walls, stiff white linen tablecloths and stiffer waiters. I shuffled my feet awkwardly outside until Mike arrived. He was a proper pop star. I got to know him quite quickly and he wasn't full of himself at all, but he did have something, a certain confidence that I hadn't seen before. He was generous but not flashy and we chatted about music and life and by the end of the meal I had agreed to be part of the Jump Off party accompanying The Streets on a UK tour in February 2005.

At each venue we staged an MC battle and the winner went in the van with the Jump Off crew to the next show. It was an innovative idea – to battle every night for the right to stay on tour. Promoters weren't convinced. This was at the height of Mike's mainstream popularity and yet they were nervous about stopping the show every night to invite rappers up on stage.

I was down with it and the format was a success. I battled every date of the tour. I didn't win every competition but always came back on at the next date and fought back through to the final. I could hardly believe it the first time I lost – the rapper's name was BJ, beating him should have been a given but Glasgow weren't being too kind to me that night. The next loss would happen in Portsmouth – or maybe it was Plymouth – and once again being a southern fairy would be my downfall. As soon as I was introduced as coming from London the crowd starting shouting 'Who are ya? Who are ya?' like it was a bloody football match.

After the tour, I began to visit Mike's studio in south west London, a shed-like structure (called the Shed) backing on to the District line in the middle of a suburban terrace. The toilet doubled up as a microphone booth, so if the bog was used I'd have to wait until the cistern had filled again before I could continue working. I had some strong tracks even at that early stage, although many would take years to get released, among them 'Just Be Good to Green' – all but the Lily Allen part, which would be added much later – and 'I Need You Tonight'. In some of my lyrics I could be a lippy little shit and that came from my time spent battling. I enjoyed being provocative. My nan didn't approve of all of my lyrics but she forgave me because she could separate the art from real life and knew how I was day-to-day. I was aware that I could come across as sexist and chauvinistic or slightly mean in my lyrics ('Don't menstruate but I am a bleedin' cunt' will always be one of my favourites), but that wasn't me in person – unless it was called for, of course.

I got to meet the people around Mike, including Ted Mayhem. He looked after The Streets' international business at Warner and the company agreed to finance Mike's own label, The Beats. Ted co-ran it with him. Although The Beats had already been working with The Mitchell Brothers I was to be the first signing. Ted said that one of the things that convinced him I had real talent and that I was a serious prospect for the label was the way I was constantly to be seen freestyling and rapping all over. But both he and Mike had confidence that I could be more than a battle rapper. The Beats' third act would be Example. As things turned out, he would be their final signing. There was a female artist, Neon Hitch, they were looking at signing, but this was later, just as the label was being shut down.

The first Beats release I was on was a verse on the remix of the Mitchell Brothers' 'Routine Check' but it didn't quite work out the way I wanted. Mike suggested that I took the opportunity to use my battling skills to cuss them all. So I did. That wasn't the problem. They treated the vocal in post-production with a plug-in that put my part slightly out of time. Nobody else could hear it, because people never do, but they'd already pressed the CD before I heard it. And to me, as a rapper, that's one of the worst things in the world – being off time. I'm a rapper, being on beat is the first rule, that's the whole point.

Spending time on tour with Mike, hanging out and seeing him work, even just going to his house, was an education. Seeing a UK rapper who was achieving creatively, making money and living a good life had opened my eyes. For the first time I could see myself making a go of music, that there was an opportunity to be grabbed to make a better life.

Now I needed a manager – or managers. I was friendly with Mike Skinner's cousin Spencer and his mate Josh, a video director whose parents owned the logistics company Stagetruck. We had a lot of fun together – Spencer and Josh had a crew from Barnet and every time we got together we'd be out all night and then back to someone's house putting the world to rights until seven in the morning. There were some wicked times but Ted made it implicitly clear that Josh and Spencer managing me wasn't going to happen. While a label couldn't dictate who would manage any artist – and shouldn't have that kind of say – they were very much against the idea. The Beats wanted someone with more experience and felt that Josh and Spencer were still finding their way and it was Tim Medcraft who introduced me to Ged Malone. In fact, we met in the same pub where I'd first got together with Tim: every Friday his company would hold drinks for their artists at the venue.

Tim insisted Ged come down to meet me and Ged says now his main memory was of a 'kid with wonky teeth and a bird on each arm and I thought... Hmm, interesting'. I was probably wearing my Avirex and Evisu again, not being too subtle about who I was. The two girls were Naoko and her younger sister Yumiko. Ged shook hands with me and he's been my manager ever since. Despite the fact that he's paid to put up with my shit, Ged has gone on to do a lot more than he needed to for me as a manager and he's become one of the most important people in my life. He was later joined by Simon Burke-Kennedy, who also became all too familiar with what a pain in the arse I can be. He's slightly more gentle than Ged but I also love him dearly and trust him implicitly – I'm lucky to have both of them in my life, as well as helping to look after my career.

I made another lasting friendship through my first press shoot for The Beats. This was Rufus, who then ran a streetwear company. I'd picked up a couple of their tees while out shopping with stylist and designer Carri Munden (of Cassette Playa). The tee was pink (brave, I know) with a repeated cloud pattern and a storm cloud with a lightning strike through it. It was probably too big but I was still slowly emerging from my XXL Akademiks tracksuit and Avirex phase. Everyone went mental about the tee when I blogged a picture of me wearing it on tour, so I reached out to his company in the hope of some freebies. Their factory was in Stamford Hill, just up the road from where I'd grown up and Rufus and I hit it off when we met. He had lived more than a lifetime already if you measure a man's age by his experiences. He began as an investment banker, then became a freelance photographer before becoming a clothes designer and company owner. He would go on to do a lot of filming and photography for me.

The shotting side of my life had remained at about the same level and I wasn't going to take it as far as I could have which, in hindsight, was probably no bad thing. There was definitely a lot more money to be made but there was also a lot more at stake and I was just beginning to see some potential in my music. There were times I'd take on ten boxes and there were times when there was a drought and I'd be lucky to get half a box. The consequences of a loss were worse when I worked on consignment, as I discovered when I was jacked. A loss was a hit on what was someone else's money – and it was quite difficult to make it back without the merchandise to sell. At my level fortunes changed in an instant and you could quickly find yourself a long way down a very dark hole. That hole finally opened under me not long after my 21st birthday with a major raid by the police.

A DAY IN THE PHONE OF PROFESSOR GREEN

5. THE BEATS

Police, in the shape of firearms squad SO19 and the Scotland Yard Kidnap Unit swarmed my mate's car. The pigs didn't identify themselves immediately and my mate, finding himself attacked by persons unknown, fought back and the police proceeded to punch him, step on him and taser him – all entirely unprovoked and uncalled for. Then they stormed the block and made for the flat.

I had moved into another mate's place, in Euston, just four days earlier. A strange and unfortunate string of events had led to something going missing and having to be paid for and this resulted in a very stressful few days trying to recover that money – for me and everyone else involved. It ended up with friends getting caught up in something that wasn't anything to do with them. It was ultimately my fault, them trying to help me and me trying to help someone else.

In short: way too many fucking links in the chain...

When the police struck we heard the commotion from the fourth floor and looked down to see the last thing any of us fucking needed. We rushed to empty the flat. The coppers stormed in, grabbing, shoving and hitting everyone, before putting us in cuffs and leaving us over bits of furniture. I found myself folded over a table leg, the table itself now on its side. They wrecked a lot of shit in their search for a firearm, their main excuse for the raid. I had Jump Off trophies that were awarded for twice winning seven weeks in a row and they were smashed because they had sealed lids. The police claimed they were looking for a firearm inside them, although the trophies were welded shut. They didn't find one, of course (though I still wonder where that bag of pills disappeared to...). The pans (scales) and all the rest of the bits and bobs had gone out of the window – I saw the scales again in the interrogation room of West End Central police station: they'd somehow survived the fall. That was when the coppers dumped a yellow drawstring bag from Modo in front of me on the table. But there was no Avirex jacket or Akademiks tracksuit in it – it was full of 'erb.

Apparently, we'd been under surveillance for three days. Yet for all that work I was released after 24 hours, although they kept all my possessions as evidence, including all the clothes I'd been wearing – even my socks – and left just my boxer shorts. Without a phone or money I couldn't call Naoko and so I walked from Savile Row in Mayfair to Camden wearing only paper overalls, the boxers and plimsolls. That was a very long three miles. The police also kept every other bit of clothing I owned which they'd taken from the flat. I was stuck in Naoko's without a phone or clothes for days until she had a day off. I wore only a pair of size 'M' Nike joggers and pretty much stayed in the one old t-shirt of mine which she had.

The realisation that I'd been under surveillance left me with a newfound paranoia. After I got home I saw a van sitting opposite Naoko's mum's and wondered what it was doing there... I'd never worried like this before – but until now I hadn't ever felt like I had shit to lose. The raid seemed to be a symbol: if I kept going down this road I'd destroy anything I might achieve with my music. I started to think about everything I hadn't thought about before. About how lucky I'd been to have shotted for years and never got touched. I saw what was in the balance. And yet one of the first things I did a few days later was jump on a bus up to Holloway to grab a box and start making some of the debt back. I didn't really feel as though it was mine to pay but although I might not have been the one to blame, I'd left a long-time friend short and wasn't going to leave it that way for long. Stupid, without a doubt, but I felt I didn't have an option. I didn't have any other viable way of making back the money and I wasn't expecting any help from anywhere else.

Taking time to look back and having learned some valuable lessons up to and including this encounter with the police, it might have been better to stop for a minute and let everything carry on around me. But I was already caught in a shit-storm and didn't have the capacity to take a step back. I could sometimes feel a bit of self-pity but generally I didn't see the point in procrastinating and feeling all hard done by. It wasn't conducive to anything apart from failure, becoming an old and bitter man and leading an unhappy life. Most of us are born hard done by. I kept going.

We're born where we're born, we try for what we try for. People don't seem to understand that they aren't owed anything but so many people go through life acting as if they are. It would have been easy for me to sit on my arse and say, 'Fuck it', and to be a victim of my circumstances. From the start, I had had to live my life without support from my parents. My dad and I weren't in contact and my relationship with my mum was poor. Their absence shaped my decisions all the way through my life, but I had come through it.

I did what I needed to do in order to survive and succeed. I was close to real achievement but everything was in danger of just sliding away. I decided to take the risk and go for it – because it was a risk to believe that I could make a real success of it, in a way.

When I got around to speaking to Skinner he said he'd write a letter for the court, if necessary. I felt a mixture of surprise, gratitude and relief. If I did go to prison he would still be around afterwards. But in the end the case went nowhere. Nobody helped the police with their enquiries and they couldn't pin anything on anyone in particular. The most anyone received was a caution, which was a shame because he didn't even deserve that.

For a while I couldn't get in touch with anyone because I didn't have a phone and I'd lost all my numbers. In any case, we didn't want to talk on the phone because we were all so fucking paranoid.

I did an interview once which ran under the headline MUSIC SAVED ME FROM A LIFE OF CRIME – but that's only half-right. I fucking hate sensationalised, bullshit headlines. It's more accurate to say that I made what was my first attempt to leave shotting behind because my heart was never in it – I was a good boy trying to be a bad man. At the same time it was also true to say I was in deep enough for it to have been all too easy for me to keep dealing. So I would go so far as to say I was glad music was there as an alternative.

Shotting isn't easy. Anyone who tells you otherwise is a fantasist or a liar. It's a fucking headache. You have to be lucky every day, you only have to be unlucky once. Just once. And then you find yourself with a knife to your throat or a gun in your face or you end up sitting in a police cell wearing paper overalls. After months of being re-bailed I picked up a phone to a number I didn't recognise and was greeted by a typical prick-on-a-power-trip type copper. 'Who's this?' I asked.

'The guy who decides whether or not to ruin the rest of your life.' Wanker. Luckily, I was left with an NFA (no further action) notice in my hand and a new way of seeing what I should be doing with my life.

At the Jump Off I had become a marked man because I did so well all the time. I was the one that up-and-coming people wanted to scalp to make their own name, but I managed to take my battling skills all the way to the Bahamas for Fight Klub, a global rap battle in October 2005. The winner was to take home $50,000 and a Cadillac. My UK qualifier battle was against Life, who rapped with Phi Life Cypher. It was a chance to showcase more of my lyrical ability rather than just a barrage of 'mum' jokes.

I arrived in the Bahamas along with the Jump Off and the first thing I did was try and find some weed. DJ Shortee Blitz and I went for a walk and a local guy must have thought we were tourists – no idea why – and asked us if we wanted anything. He then drove us to what looked like a row of crack houses and we got the feeling that this was somewhere we really shouldn't have been. Not a good idea to jump in a car with someone you've just met to go and get something to smoke in the Bahamas. Or anywhere. Our driver started walking from door to door while I sat tensely in the car, wondering what was going to come next – fortunately he returned with a bag and dropped us right back at the hotel.

The pre-battle meeting featured all the favourites. And me. The other guys carried weight: 2004's champion and $50,000 winner Jin, Serius Jones and Axel, who was making a lot of noise and had a development deal with Eminem's Shady Records. I was a long way from home and potentially quite out of my depth.

We headed into a room meant for a crowd of 200 that heaved with 500 fans. Among them were Busta Rhymes and 50 Cent. When the battles started, I could hear the crowd talking. 'Who's this white guy?'... 'He's from England?!'... 'Fuck's he doing here?' And to be honest, even I thought they had a point. I was far from home turf and more importantly my home crowd. My far smaller group of supporters was made up of Harry and Ara from the Jump Off, Natalie, who had come to document my attempt (only to find out the organisers wouldn't let her film), Spencer and Josh, Shortee Blitz, music journalist Hattie Collins and DJ Semtex.

But I made short work of Axel in the quarter-final and, amazingly, the crowd got behind me – I was as surprised by their reaction as anyone. Jin had an automatic bye to the final because he'd won last time and so I was up against Serius Jones in the semi-final when the judges tried to stiff me.

Serius had beaten Jin a few weeks before – and this was at a time when nobody beat Jin – there was serious money on a rematch happening between the two. Whatever the reason, I was mid-flow when the ref abruptly stopped me. He drew a line in the ring with his finger – an imaginary border between our two sides that was to stop us getting in each other's faces. At least, that was his excuse. The practical upshot was that I had to re-start my performance and anyone who raps knows how hard it is to get back into the swing of things. With the pressure of the contest I couldn't do it. Serius was declared the winner.

But the crowd wasn't having any of it. They loudly contested the dodgy decision with chants of 'UK! UK! UK!' and 'One more round!' The referee had no choice but to let us go one more time and he said the judges would allow each of us 30 seconds. Even then, Serius was given at least a minute-and-a-half as the judges listened hopefully to him drivel on and on in a desperate search for a punchline that never came. Then I got up there and spat 30 seconds, no filler, and buried him. I was through to the final.

I did all right against Jin in the first couple of rounds but by the third I was fucking up. I was a bit intimidated and I was tired – I'd been battling all night while he'd just been sitting there, no doubt stacking up lines while he was waiting. He took his second title and I had to wave goodbye to $50,000. The money would have been welcome (even with the exchange rate) but fuck knows what I would have done with the Cadillac.

Back home I was finding it hard to see that maybe I was having too much fun with my more recent mates. They were different to the people I'd known before. I guess we were just partying too hard. That phase went on for a while and I remember at one point Mike saying, 'You're hanging out with the wrong people.' And something about the way he said it really resonated. He was referring particularly to the Barnet crowd that I knew through Spencer and Josh. I mean, the house we'd often party at was nicknamed the Death Pad. Things sometimes got a bit dark as I was beginning to experiment beyond weed. And I realised that Mike was only telling me it was possible to enjoy myself without it becoming my whole life. And it was true, I had been getting a bit lazy with my songwriting, I was becoming sidetracked by going out too much and I had slowed down my work. I decided it was time to knock it on the head. And that was more or less the whole story with me and the recreationals for a while. Unfortunately, that change in thinking marked the beginning of the end of my relationship with Naoko.

Spenny and Josh hadn't become my managers in the end but they did take me out on tour once as support for Sway when he released *This is My Demo*. We were travelling around on sofas in the back of a transit, which might sound like a giggle but was for the most part absolutely fucking freezing! I think Jonah was DJ'ing for me then and David/Alpha came along, as well as Alex and Chyna. It was Spenny's birthday the night of the Liverpool Academy concert in February and so a party followed and I'm pretty sure they both carried on long after everyone else finished. They had business elsewhere the next day and left before seeing anyone but had to get back to take us to Barrow-in-Furness – a strange place, but we'll get to that.

It was getting late in the day and we hadn't heard from Josh or Spencer and both of their phones were ringing out. We began to worry they'd had a road accident. It wasn't looking likely that we'd make the next gig when all of a sudden we got a call – they'd pulled off the motorway for a quick nap but ended up sleeping for hours. They made it back in time to just about get us to Barrow for the show (driving at the legal speed limit, of course). After the performance, just as we were leaving the stage, we were asked – as a collective – if *we* were Sway. Strange question, as he was, last time I looked, one man. I got the impression not many people made it to Barrow to perform. It seemed quite removed from civilisation and had a distinct sense of eeriness about it – at night anyway. Not helped by all the huge BAE military works there.

My first release on The Beats was *Lecture #1* in March 2006. It had been something I'd been working towards before I was signed, almost without realising it. The mixtape was a collection of tunes, freestyles from the radio and gigs and glimpses of songs to come. 'Before I Die' and 'Upper Clapton Dance' would become my calling cards.

The transition from stage to working in a recording studio had not been straightforward. Battling, playing gigs and recording whole songs each required different skills. I had to keep up with my habit of writing lyrics to get enough for an entire track and as a result my way of making sense of the writing process was to sit with a beat playing on repeat and write rhymes with whatever came to mind. In doing so I was beginning to find a way to express myself. Seeing my thoughts on paper helped me understand my feelings.

There was a strong stigma attached to battle-rapping which is that battle rappers generally lack the substance to carry a song, much less a whole album. Their big mistake is to take the same approach to songs as they would do to battles, rather than sustaining a mood or creating a vibe. Punchlines can have a place in a song, the best of them fitting into the overall concept, but there has to be more to a song to make it work. Not every battler has fallen at this hurdle, of course

– think Jay-Z, DMX, Biggie and Busta Rhymes – but perhaps in their day it was just more common to make the leap.

My rhymes were inspired by the way I grew up. By what was going on at the time. Rhyming helped me deal with things, it was a form of therapy for me at times, helping me get what was inside out – and, more importantly, onto a piece of paper where I could make sense of it. I've often felt relief when I've finished a song – much as I'm sure my managers and everyone at my label do, but for very different reasons. It's important to learn a form of expression, whatever it may be, and for me it was writing raps. It gave me a voice and, more importantly, an outlet. Writing gave me something positive to focus on. It wouldn't be rap for everyone: for some people it was painting, for others it was dance or design – any of the many ways in which a person can express themselves. It's useful to have an avenue for the anger, the sadness and the upset and to be able to let go and channel that negative energy, rather than bottling emotions and feelings which then come out more unpredictably and dangerously. My most successful songs have come from the harder times in my life. That said, it's important not to become self-destructive in a search for a match to re-light that fire.

Get a thought down on paper and make it into a good idea – that was one of the many things that Mike Skinner taught me. 'There's no such thing as a bad idea,' he'd say. I disagreed; for instance, another visit to the Death Pad would have been a bad idea. Mike helped me to think differently and to consider melody and song structure. He had song-writing theory books but they weren't, to be honest, for me and I never looked at them. I always did my own thing and I was confident about it, even back then. The first line I came out with for a song might not be great, but I'd keep going. I figured that if I hadn't got something down to work with, I'd got nothing. A page full of anything, no matter what, was better than a page full of nothing. To state the obvious, nothing's ever finished if it isn't started.

At times it can be it easy to start second-guessing everything, to the point where I don't even put a line on paper, my mind wanders and before I know it I'm off watching YouTube videos of animals dubbed with humorous human voices instead. It's better to rip whole pages out and chuck them in the bin than it is to write nothing. There have been a few songs that I've scribbled out on a napkin, fully formed in 20 minutes and others that have taken months to come together. It can take a while for emotions to accumulate in a song with a coherent shape that means something to the people listening to it and not just me.

And where does an idea come from? Anywhere. Anything. Alex's mum was listening to Classic FM and Brahms' 'Hungarian Dance No 5' came on. Alex immediately sampled it and put the beat together, sent it to me with the file name 'Upper Clapton Dance' and I sent him the chorus pretty much straight back – everything aligned nicely. 'Before I Die' reflects some of the comedy I grew up with – it's basically an aural bucket list. On the remix of 'Before I Die', I had Big Narstie and Ghetts alongside Plan B and Example. I had met Ghetts on the first Streets tour I did when I was battling, as Kano was supporting and Ghetts and Demon were rolling with him.

When I first heard the beat Skinner made for 'Stereotypical Man', I thought, I kind of like this, but what the fuck is it? Is this rap? But it was just Mike Skinner. Everyone can put their own twist on things but not many people have it in them to create their own sound and that's something that he still has. I sent him a version of the track with just me on it, rapping the chorus rather than singing. He sent it back with Leo the Lion singing it instead. It had become something more than just a rap song. In a way, it was ahead of its time because there wasn't really such a thing as commercial UK rap. 'Stereotypical Man' got played but there was a bit of resistance from the more hardcore DJs who didn't like its melodic hook. But then it was playlisted at 1Xtra. I had great support from DJs even back then: Semtex, MistaJam, Zane Lowe, MK, Shortee Blitz (and at the time Big Ted) and others too.

The clip for 'Stereotypical Man' featured a girl named Tia, who I started seeing regularly after an initial couple of dates. I had split up with Naoko by now and although Tia and I had started seeing each other some time later, Naoko happened to be the make-up artist for the 'Stereotypical Man' video, which was a dark coincidence. I wasn't in any hurry to get together with someone new as I'd just come out of such a long and meaningful relationship. I actually reached out to Naoko, I remember it being on a Sunday. We hadn't spoken in ages but I felt like before I got too deep into anything else it deserved another shot – we'd been through too much to just walk away. We arranged to meet up later that evening, but then she called back in tears saying, 'I know you've been seeing someone else.' My pride got in the way of me making any explanations – I didn't feel I owed her any.

I later found out that that Spencer's missus at the time, Charlotte, had told Naoko that I'd had a date with Tia. I had no idea why Charlotte thought it was her business – it would have been more kind for Naoko to have heard the news directly from me. But I didn't deal with Naoko's anger very well. My stubbornness led to her not talking to me for more than four years. Losing touch with her sister Yumiko, or Yumi, also hurt. I completely understood and never resented her for it – she had to stick by her sis, but during those few years I'd been with Naoko, Yumi and I had become like brother and sister ourselves.

If anything, that dramatic conclusion to the story with Naoko only speeded up the beginning of my relationship with Tia and we ended up staying together for a couple of years. My nan didn't really take much of a liking to her – she even said she was going to push her down the stairs once, although she didn't have the physical build for it. Or the temperament – but she is cockney, so you always had to be careful.

As the music side of my life seemed to be taking off I decided to leave Select. I had become even more disengaged from the mundane work as I did more with The Beats. I was still a good worker when I put my mind to it, but there were a lot of late, late nights one way or another and that led to a lot of tired mornings at the office not concentrating on the screen. I know my nan regretted my decision but 'that talking music', as she called rap, eventually won out. Nan had supported me however she could, even coming to gigs to see me live, once she'd realised how important my music was to me, but I knew she would have been happier to see me in a regular job. Sorry, Nan. In fact now's probably a good time to say thank you to Joe, Colin, Les, Paul, Michael, Mark, Nick, Steve and everyone at Select Typesetters; thank you for putting up with me, and for giving me a chance when no one else would.

MistaJam booked me for UK Takeover 4 in Nottingham in May. I met his friend – producer Joe Buddha and through him I met Cleo. They've all gone on to become my Nottingham fam and I've had a lot of good nights in the city, not least the night, when Radio 1Xtra were broadcasting live from the event. After one too many Jack n'cokes I started to use words the BBC weren't all that comfortable about. In the end, MistaJam came out and put me in a headlock live on stage and that was the end of that. There was another night in Nottingham when I was stood at the side of stage with Skinny just as Wiley was about to perform. Wiley asked me if he could bring me out to do a freestyle and I said, 'Allow it, bro, I'm mashed.' Wiley performed three songs and then introduced me as England's best freestyler – not sure I lived up to the introduction. I've made a lot of friends in a lot of cities we've been to over the years.

Around the same time I gained both a friend and a new place to live. The friend was of the four-legged variety – I'd been after a dog for a while and when I was sitting at my computer on MSN one morning, I saw a friend, Ellie, had changed her status to 'Does anyone want to buy a staffie?' I met the dog at the place she shared with Hannah, who had called the dog Boss. This was not a good idea. I didn't want a dog to think they're the boss or even Boss. So when I bought him I changed his name to Alfie. He was up for grabs because Hannah worked full-time and Ellie didn't think their home could accommodate a dog left on his own. But within a week, the third room in the house had become available, both me and the former Boss took it immediately and we stayed put for the next 18 months or so. I had some great adventures in Stratford – or Stratty Castle, as we ended up calling it.

I didn't get on that well with Hannah – mostly trivial stuff like her not doing the washing up as regularly – but Ellie and I developed a brother-sister relationship. She says now that she thinks we were both struggling a bit in our lives and that's why we connected. I had just been going through a rough patch with my nan and that was why I had to move out in a hurry – Nan had not given me much option. Ellie and I got close quickly after we started house-sharing, although we'd always had eventful times together, from the very start of our friendship.

I met Ellie through MySpace, while she was living in Burton in the Midlands. The very first time I went for a night out with her after she came down to London I met her at Stratford station on our way to Cargo in Shoreditch. As we climbed the stairs we passed a couple of guys and one of them muttered something to me in east European-accented English that didn't sound very complimentary. I said, 'Yeah, mate, whatever, have a good night.' Then, speaking more clearly, he addressed Ellie: 'Blonde bitch.' Ah, okay. I had my hand in my pocket and I took hold of my key between my fingers – I didn't have anything else on me. As he approached me I thought I'd take the initiative and hit him first. As I did he basically star-jumped – touch. I turned to face the other guy who was absolutely massive but fortunately he just stammered out an apology on his friend's behalf. The encounter got me off to a good start with Ellie.

We bonded even more when we lived together and we got up to a lot of mischief all the time. One normal Tuesday night, Tia had just gone to bed and I sat up with Ellie watching TV. She jokingly suggested we get some mandy, so I said, 'Cool, I'll make the call while you're driving.' She said, 'Cool, grab your jacket and I'll get the car keys' – it was one of those situations where we kept calling each other's bluff, encouraging each other. We drove to north London and grabbed a gram then headed back home, took a large dab, waited and – nothing. We had a smoke, decided to call it a night and each went off to our bedrooms. I crept into bed quietly so that I didn't disturb Tia. She stirred, turned over and cuddled into me. And at that precise moment I came up. I texted Ellie, 'Are your covers feeling a bit better than normal?' Back came the message, 'I'm. Off. My. Nut.' But I couldn't get out of bed because I would have disturbed Tia so I had to lie there until I could eventually get to sleep. That was very typical of the house-share with Ellie – there was a lot of stupid behaviour like that, lots of Nando's and a fair few bottles of cheap rosé wine.

There was one Sunday when Ellie and I started off at the house having an all-day session with my mate Neon Hitch (the singer-songwriter who came on tour with The Beats and was almost signed by them) and her best friend Violetta. We made a last-minute decision to make the journey into Shoreditch to the Hoxton Kitchen where there was some kind of live music event going on. But they wouldn't let me in. Ellie and I had ourselves been up all night and all day by now and devilish inspiration struck me. I jokingly told the guy on the door, 'This is the girl from N-Dubz.' But he took me totally seriously and the attitude immediately changed. N-Dubz weren't yet mainstream at that point and I'd stumbled on a massive fan – even if he clearly wasn't quite a big enough fan to know what Tulisa looked like. He was all over us, 'Oh my god, respect! I love your music, you're doing your thing!' he said to Ellie. Ellie had no idea of who she was supposed to be.

In fairness, Ellie and Tulisa look nothing alike. I hadn't expected the response we got. Ellie held it together, probably as much to see how far we could take the joke as anything else. We had almost got in, but then the guy running it asked for Ellie's autograph. Trying not to laugh, I could see her freeze as pen and paper were produced. She didn't even know she was 'Tulisa', much less how spell it – and just forget about 'Contostavlos' – but she played along by writing a squiggle that could have been anything. Ellie whispered, 'Stephen! What are you doing?' but, making it up as we went, I just encouraged her to play along.

We were invited through to the back and I wasn't ready to let the joke go just yet. 'Maybe you should get up on stage!' I said, in earshot of the people whose event it was. My suggestion went down a treat with everyone except Ellie. They were all over us thinking That-Girl-From-N-Dubz would do something spontaneously. 'Oh, yeah! You really should!' I think Ellie was probably ready to kill me but we stayed just long enough to get wrecked before we did a runner. It was an unusually busy night for a Sunday and I made sure that Ellie was That-Girl-From-N-Dubz to everyone we met.

I could be myself around Ellie and Ellie was herself around me (when she wasn't being Tulisa). We were also, along with Hannah, blond-haired and pale and were often taken as Polish, although that wasn't such a deliberate thing. We lived on quite a mixed cultural street and as there was a big Polish community everyone just assumed we were part of it. Even the Poles talked to us in Polish and we'd just smile, nod and get on with it. Ellie would joke I was tanorexic as I'd use sunbeds almost as much as she would, just round the corner at the Polish-owned salon. The truth was the sunbeds just helped the effects of my acne and my eczema. Fortunately, my acne has since fucked off and needless to say I haven't been on a sunbed in years. Although... I could probably do with one.

Throughout the silliness Ellie and I always had each other's backs and we made sure that the danger was always the right kind, at least when it was just the two of us. When others were involved it wasn't always so simple. There was one time when Ellie had gone out around 11 pm to do the usual wine top-up run and I got a panicked phone call from her just after she'd left. I found out the details later – she'd just left the house and had been heading towards the corner shop at the end of the road, just as we did every day. There was an African family living opposite us who we'd not had any run-ins with. But that night, this guy came out of their house, stood in front of Ellie and wouldn't let her pass. She crossed the road and walked around him and she heard a cough. She turned around to see if he'd gone, but he was facing her, staring silently. Ours was a quiet back street that cars very rarely passed and she made a dash for the shop where she called me.

I ran down immediately with Alfie in tow and saw nobody on my way. A spooked Ellie was waiting for me and, as we paid, and made our way out the guy emerged from nearby bushes where he'd been waiting for her. Ellie still reminds me of that night, which soon became known in our adventures as the night I saved her from a mass murderer. Maybe not – we'll never really know – but it was fucking freaky.

You wouldn't have been able to tell from my daily life which, aside from encounters with mass murderers, remained fairly ordinary, that I had tracks on rotation on the BBC and was frequently working with Mike Skinner in his studio. I had a track I'd worked on from my time in Holloway called 'Nothing More' which Westwood played but it didn't get a release – not all of my stuff did. Thinking back, I should have spent more time making mixtapes and keeping up being creative. It wasn't a conscious decision but I didn't add as much to my catalogue as I could have. It was the same with another song I liked,

'Running to the Exit', for which we even shot a video and there are remixes that I smashed which people still talk and tweet about now – of The Streets' 'When You Wasn't Famous' from 2006 and The Twang's 'Either Way' the next year – which show the depth of what I was doing.

Mike himself worked all the fucking time and our relationship was always tightly focused on the music. We were always taking songs apart, talking over the tracks, deconstructing choruses. Our times in the studio were full of good conversation, but we had conflicting ideas for my trajectory as an artist. He had a vision for who he wanted me to be and I just wanted to be myself. He wanted to take control of everything. The Mitchell Brothers' early stuff, to my ears, sounds a bit too much like Mike and I didn't want my tracks to sound like they were from a Streets album. While a lot of what he added to my songs was incredible our differing views meant we sometimes ended up at loggerheads.

Whenever I've not gone with my gut feeling, I've found that I usually regretted the decision. A certain amount of creative friction can be healthy and a push-back from Mike helped me define my ideas in my own mind. But it could be really hard work. I do remember one email from Mike I'll always appreciate. He wrote that he'd spent too long trying to make me into the rapper he thought I should be as opposed to making the most of the rapper I was. This dynamic had slowed us down but now we knew it we were finally pulling in the same direction. The sad thing was that pretty soon after we found common ground, the parent company Warner pulled the financing and by the end of 2007 The Beats was over. It was a shame; we were just getting into our stride.

The end didn't entirely come as a surprise. We'd had some

good times but while Ted was trying to hold everything together and keep the show going, we were all making it up as we went along. I liked that about The Beats. It was honest. Everyone was a liability, everything was very likely to go wrong and it took a lot of luck for anything to go the way we hoped it would.

Touring was an example. Ted drove us and would navigate – in those pre-sat nav days entirely by the Force, real Jedi mind tricks. When you're touring, with so many people on top of each other, everyone trying to work and also trying to have a good time, things are bound to happen. On one tour in those early days we were in Liverpool, I think, and someone asked me for a condom. I'd given him the only one I had, but he struck out with that particular lady and later, in a reversal of fortunes, I ended up having to ask for it back. We were all staying in the same room, and I think Alex was in there with a girl too, so I went into the bathroom. Anyone else still around was hopefully asleep. Or at least under the duvet with their fingers in their ears.

On another tour I ended up making friends with a girl called Rachelle who at the time worked for Matt at Lovedough, a regular night at Digital in Newcastle. We went for an after-party and were spoilt rotten. Samurai was DJing for me at the time (We got our own radio show as part of BBC Radio 1's 'In New DJs We Trust' in early 2007. Charlotte Coker, who I'd met at Kiss, got us in to do a demo and we got through.) and Chyna and Alex were also about. Despite getting into a mess – Chyna nearly had a drunken fight with security and I had to make myself sick when I got back to the hotel to avoid the room spinning – I've kept in regular contact with Rachelle ever since. It's scary how quick ten years pass.

Both Example and I played on the early 2007 leg of Plan B's

'Who Needs Actions When You Got Words' tour and that led to a very useful link for me. Mark Surridge was then my tour manager, although not for long. I had met him through Naoko and we quickly became good mates. Example eventually stole him from me for a while, although Mark now works with Ed Sheeran in some capacity, I don't quite know what it is he does – I think he's basically an after-party organiser, not a job I'd mind doing, to be honest. Chyna, Jonah and Alex also came along on the Plan B tour.

We were in a city down south when I came off stage and someone handed me something in foil and said, 'Have a look at that.' People often handed me weed or offered me a spliff due to my association with greenery so I didn't think much of it until I got upstairs to the dressing room and had a look. When I saw what it was I immediately ran back downstairs to try and find the bloke and luckily I did. I put in an order and he arrived at the next stop with it and so began a long relationship – a long-distance relationship, actually, as he lived fucking miles away, but the journey seemed worth it. People would pay £10 a gram for this stuff (the standard price now but back then eighths were still between 3 and 3.5 grams and cost a score – £20).

The rest of that tour featured terribly bad weather and I remember once seeing a huge truck tyre hurtling down the other side of the motorway. There was lots of listening to whatever the new Jay-Z album was at the time and then there was getting entirely carried away on the last night in Southampton. Lewis came along with a pal who brought a pocket full of fun and, along with Example and Fat Daz (who sold merchandise for Plan B and became a permanent fixture in my circle of friends), we all got thoroughly involved before being separated for our journeys home. It wasn't the most comfortable ride home in our cramped Ford people-carrier.

It wasn't uncommon for Example, Plan B and I to be mucking about. One night after one of Example's launches we ended up at the 333 bar in Hoxton. I'd just stood up to book a cab home when someone pushed past me, stepping all over me and clearly out of his head. I laughingly said, 'Watch it, mate.' I began to walk away but he came back, giving it. 'What did you say?' he asked. I had only been having a giggle before but now I was more serious when I told him to watch himself. He instantly ran over and grabbed his mate. I told 'em both to stop being fucking silly and assumed that would be that – it wasn't.

I was now stood outside the doors to the main room at the top of the stairs and was on the phone to Addison Lee. No sooner had the lady asked, 'Cash or account?' when the doors came flying open with Plan B caught in a headlock by security and one of the blokes I'd argued with, less well-restrained and still trying to hit Ben. I went for the guy but we all got flung down the stairs and kicked out. I chucked my brown leather Avirex to Tia and ran round the corner.

Example was now quite a way down the road towards Hoxton Square dealing with one of the blokes, of which there were now three, and Plan B and I took on the other two. B then managed to twist his ankle and he started laughing, at which point we stopped, said, 'Look – we're not gonna kill each other…', shook hands and had a laugh at our stupid behaviour. It wasn't hard for B or me to do that as we'd not taken so much as a punch. But we looked down the road to see Example still laying in to the bloke he was fighting. He came out on top but unfortunately took one just under the eye and ended his night at Homerton A&E being stitched up. One of my more honest encounters with violence – a straightforward tear-up.

But for sheer stupidity, The Beats Tour of July 2007 topped everything, including my own live outings. And I am someone – it has been said – who likes to loosen up a bit before my gigs. As well as during. And after. Friends might, with justification, point to the time I stayed up all night before a Jump Off final, among numerous other occasions. But that was nothing compared with what became known as the H2E tour, thanks to a certain crystalline powdery substance that we'd mix into random water bottles in the dressing room fridges when we arrived at the venues. Now all of that was over.

Looking back at the The Beats I'd say I hadn't helped things in those times when I didn't make it easy, when I didn't deliver music. But I wasn't working to any kind of system and I didn't have a way of guaranteeing that I would come up with finished tracks. Mike, on the other hand, had spent months in the USA with Warner, watching the big hip-hop producers at work. He was making a lot of beats. And then there was Example, who definitely made the most out of his time at The Beats. I guess he was the most competent at the time and was the most productive as far as producing material and understanding the graft. Example has always been a great businessman. He has always worked fucking hard and we've gone on to become close mates.

We did pretty well. On other occasions major labels like Warners have spent a lot more money on side projects and come out with a lot less to show for it than The Beats did. And I think it's a testament both to Mike's musical and A&R skills that he saw something in me and Example that did have staying power. We stuck at it, hammered on and made something of it.

But the fact was that we had been caught in a squeeze in the music industry. Everyone was bringing things in-house. Mike's original label was 679 and that went back to Warner. All of a sudden people just weren't outsourcing anything thanks to the collapse in sales caused by torrent sites like Napster. The bottom line was the bottom line: the numbers didn't add up. Warner spent a lot of money and they were making fuck-all. It wasn't a personal issue; they just saw us as a big hole. The immediate concern for me was that all my unreleased material remained the property of Warner, including 'Just Be Good to Green' and 'I Need You Tonight'. It would be a long time before I saw them again.

And that was the end of The Beats. I still have nothing but love and respect for Mike and I always reach out because we have the same birthday. But I didn't hear from him for a long time. I think he went through a lot of shit after The Beats went south. I know I did.

6. IF I EVER SEE YOU AGAIN

I didn't quite go back to square one with my music after The Beats folded, but it was close.

People assumed, particularly in the area in which I grew up, that you're making good money once you've started signing deals, getting radio play and that kind of thing. In my case that simply wasn't true. The Beats had been a side project so technically I was still signed to Warner and it would take me a year and cost me a fair amount in lawyers' fees to get them to release me and songs that would eventually make it on to my first album, *Alive Till I'm Dead*. Mike's manager Tim Vigon was one of those who did help. He campaigned on my behalf to Warner. He was well-respected in the industry so when he weighed in, people listened. But in the immediate aftermath of The Beats folding I couldn't do much to capitalise on the audience I'd built up. Time was passing and my name was fading away.

At 24 I wasn't even young any more. Jay-Z might have released his first album, *Reasonable Doubt*, when he was 26 and in danger of being outdone by new blood – Biggie and Nas were younger and released debut records before him – but I wasn't kidding myself that I was the next Jay-Z.

I did the rounds of the record companies with Ged. We had meetings with Virgin, Sony and Warner themselves but nothing came of them apart from a lot of hot air. Maybe I had a reserve of self-belief that kept me going. Maybe it was blind stupidity. Or a bit of both. But even though there were many moments when I felt like saying, 'Fuck it, this is a waste of my fucking time,' I kept on regardless. When you're in a bad situation you can either focus on the positive or on the negative and I've always been quite good at making light of the dark.

I ended up signing a deal with an indie label that was a sister to my publishers, Bucks. I got a very small advance which I used to finance videos to go with 'Upper Clapton Dance' and 'Hard Night Out' from *Lecture #1*. But I needed cash to live on and there was very little of that. The label were mainly unhelpful. I remember one email from them to Ged saying there was to be no other money after the videos, that the money was to pay for the music and my finances were of no concern to them. So I had an advance of which not a penny went in my pocket – but if I didn't have money to live on, how was I going to make any music? They seemed to care very little about my well-being and to be honest I'd thought better of Tim Medcraft than that. But he and I have since got over that and we're cool now – just a bit less cool than I once thought we were.

I made music for myself while I lived with Ellie and Hannah in Stratford. My uncle helped me build a makeshift vocal booth out of planks of thick wood. It was downstairs and the room looked liked someone had stuck a garden shed in it. I put the soundproofing in myself – it was all DIY stuff and I recorded quite a few tracks including one with Wretch, who I'd known for a long time. I found new friends too, who I would later work with, even if at the time not so much seemed to be happening. On my 24th birthday I met Aidan (Scribbler) and Anthony (Rinse) through the guy who would produce 'Just Be Good To Green' – Semothy Jones. I also met ex-boyband member Haydon who would later go on to tour with me for a short while before joining the *Thriller* cast on Shaftesbury Avenue. He later provided vocals for 'Forever Falling' on my second album. But out on my own in Stratford I was even uncertain about whether I was going to stay in music and at one point, I started to use Twitter to give away good songs that had been destined for *Lecture #2* – 'Open All Hours', 'A Problem' and 'Ballers is Bouncing'.

Twitter giveaways weren't going to pay the bills and there was only one thing I could think of that would. I was going to go back to what I'd done before to support myself. Except this time I wasn't only dealing in weed. Weed had become much harder to sell for a profit thanks to packs being sprayed with some weird sandy shit which we'd later find out was silica. It was at that point prices started to creep up. Nowadays the price of a box has pretty much doubled. I used to pay £3k on each import if I took ten and nowadays you'd be looking at £6k and above for decent bits.

I got to thinking that while I might not be able to get the music business interested in my sonic product there was another kind of merchandise that I could sell in that world for more than the weed and for which there was always demand.

It just went in a different hole. I was, I knew, moving to another level, one that I hadn't gone near before. Weed was different. Weed was a special case. I've never believed that it should be controlled in the way it is.

Now I was going to be more mercenary in my dealing, but I still felt as if I didn't have any choice. Getting a job would have meant more or less giving up on the music. Weed took up too much space and, most of all, fucking stunk. Other stuff was much easier to work with and, although the penalties were harsher, there was less that could go wrong. I bought myself a 50cc moped and then a Yamaha R125 and created another tidy little business. I was moving in mostly media and modelling circles that were very safe. I would have had to be stopped in transit for anything bad to happen and the chances of that were slim. When it did happen it was with weed.

I was on my way from Stratford to Woodford with half a bar. Rug was giving me a lift in his BMW and I had originally put the weed inside my jacket but it was too visible so, as we drove away, I pulled it out and stashed it under my seat in the front. I looked up just in time to see a police vehicle passing us but I didn't pay much attention as they hadn't slowed down and we were heading in the opposite direction.

At the next lights I looked in the wing mirror and all I could see was white. Police van. They followed us for a bit and then signalled us to pull over. Fuck. I told Rug, 'Don't say anything, they don't know where we've come from – if you get out before I do, clean the house out.' I wasn't registered as living in Stratford and a check on the car would bring up Rug's address.

The police strolled up to the window on my side. 'What are you doing around here?' the officer asked, 'picking up drugs?' I managed to cough out a laugh. I said that my mate had come to fetch me from my girlfriend's. They wanted to know what he was doing with such a nice car. I answered for him, as truthfully as I could, trying to be friendly. 'Oh, his mum's well off,' I said as if I was confiding in them. They persisted, asking again what a car registered to Woodford was doing a few miles south in Stratford. I could only repeat my story.

Rug was asked to step out of the car and the police checked the plates again. My turn came to get out. I thought, It's done. They searched me. They searched the car, everywhere. Except – unbelievably – under the front seat. We were allowed to drive on. I got to Woodford, dropped the half-bar off and I had a fucking huge spliff to calm myself down.

Near-misses aside, getting back into dealing wasn't so bad, particularly handling the other stuff. There were worse things to do than selling drugs to model bookers. I got invited to some great parties and I was making connections with talented people I would go on to work with. There was a stylist named Chris Benns I met at an Example gig in the Old Blue Last, an Old Street pub. Chris went on to be an integral part of my team for years, a trusted friend and work partner, part of my support network as well as being involved in the debauchery – he got me out of a few pickles, as well as getting into a few with me too. We were lads who got up to a lot of mischief together. But while being one of the loveliest blokes in the world, Chris had a façade that was shaped by having worked in the fashion world. He had the ability to be incredibly rude to people! He did it in quite a funny fashion but he was rude all the same. In his defence, the fashion industry is a vicious one. As I have spent more time around fashion myself I've come to realise that this is basically just how people are in that business – rude. But it made me uncomfortable and I think eventually he got the idea that it wasn't the best way to be.

Chris worked on the two independent videos I produced and his girlfriend at the time was in 'Hard Night Out'. She was a model and introduced me to her model friends, which was a welcome bonus to my friendship with the two of them. But the reality of the situation was that, even though I was still producing music on my own terms, I was drifting while the legal business with Warner rumbled on and I couldn't get to the songs that should have been mine.

By this time I hadn't seen my father for more than six years, not since my 18th birthday, after which he hadn't got in touch again and I didn't make the first move for years, just because I always had done before. But I hadn't imagined that we would never meet again. It was a cherished idea, a daydream I guess, that someday we might patch things up. The dream disappeared in April 2008 with the shocking news of his death. I had moved back to live with my nan in Woodford, the same place I had been when Edie passed. It was a Wednesday morning and Nan came to my bedroom door, crying. I sensed immediately what had happened. 'Stephen,' she said, 'your dad's dead. He hanged himself.'

I went from being completely asleep to completely awake in a millisecond and lay there in bed in shock. My first reaction was how selfish it was. Selfish because his action robbed us of that chance of re-establishing our relationship. That had been a source of comfort, even of security – the idea that in the future we, as two men, could make right the things that were wrong. As long as he was alive that was possible and now he'd taken that hope away. He hadn't been taken in a freak accident, it wasn't that someone had killed him: he had made a decision.

I got up, dressed, spoke to Ged and went to see my mate Tom to try and make sense of it all. But his suicide was incomprehensible and the anger shaded into confusion and grief that would stay with me for a long, long time.

I thought back to the last words I had said to him. It had been the previous Christmas when I had finally reached out to him. We arranged to meet after Boxing Day and the day before I gave him a shout to make arrangements. I phoned him while I was with Tia in Burger King in Walthamstow, a throwback in a way to many early memories of being with him. As a kid we would often meet in McDonald's with his new family. I felt that familiar anxiety as I waited for him to answer, like a gaping hole in my stomach.

He was living in Brentwood and I at the time had no mode of transport so I asked him if he was going to drive over to me. He replied, 'Oh, Jackie and the kids are really excited about seeing you.'

Something inside me snapped. I didn't want to see Jackie and the kids. This meeting was to have been about me and him sitting down as adults after years without seeing each other and actually sorting things out, not playing happy families. I was adult enough now to tell him what I actually felt rather than bottle it up and I let fly.

He started to stutter a reply when I finished but I cut him off.

'You know what?' I said. 'Fuck you. If I ever see you again, I'm gonna knock you out.' I disconnected the call.

But painful as that exchange was, I wouldn't change it. I deserved to be that angry: if I'd seen him, I might well have hit him because he'd hurt me so much and pushed me to a point where I couldn't respond rationally any more. Of course, I also regretted the words in another way. I had just felt so much anger and hurt that I lost control. So much was now forever left unresolved. It had been stupid not to reach out to him purely as a matter of pride. He'd known I was working with Mike and I would have loved to share all that positivity with him but I didn't and I don't even know if he ever heard my music. I loved him so much – you treasure and long for the things you can't have all the more – and now he was gone.

I went to my dad's house with Ged. Jackie and her kids were there and although we hadn't had a positive relationship up to now, I tried to be as supportive as I could. We went to Brentwood hospital but none of the family felt up to the task of identifying the body. Jackie was about to let my dad's former boss do it but I didn't agree with her doing it. The situation began to remind me of the aftermath of Nanny Edie's death. I hadn't felt able to stay with her long enough to say goodbye. I suddenly knew I had to see my dad. I was an adult and the responsibility was on me. And so it was me who approached his body as it lay on a hard, cold table with bruises around the neck. This was my first sight of him in years. I broke down.

I didn't blame Jackie for what he did – I had never got on with her but my relationship with her was separate and I recognised that. When I was little she had caused me problems by making me feel uncomfortable and by not exactly encouraging my dad to spend time with me, but his suicide wasn't her fault. While I didn't want to see anyone on her side of the family I knew we had to be in contact after his death. To blank them would have just made an awful situation worse. So when it came to the funeral, I was polite with her throughout and I did what I could to make things easier, at least until we could once again live our lives separately.

I thought about his suicide for a long time afterwards. The fact that he had done it surprised me, because I'd always seen him as a weak person and I didn't think that taking your own life was easy. I can't imagine the strength it would take to make a decision so final and I am sure that even those people who do take that leap must, in the last moments of life, wish that they could undo the knot. But maybe that's just me. No matter how bad life has got, I've always had hope. There's always the chance for things to get better. Kill yourself and you erase that chance. I could see now that this was the difference between people who end up killing themselves and people who don't. Hope.

I talked to Ken, the friend of my father who shared a house with him when I was young, in the weeks after my dad's death. I'd always liked Ken, he was a nice guy who was always the one Nanny Edie reached out to if I needed help getting in contact with my dad. He explained to me that my father had been under a lot of stress financially, having got into debt trying to keep up with the demands of family life.

Ken told me that my dad hadn't been happy. That came as another surprise to me as my dad had always seemed upbeat and jolly. I began to realise that it's often people who outwardly appear the most content who are hiding an inner darkness. This was the first time I'd realised he'd been depressed and the first time I was truly aware of how depression manifested itself, what it could mean and what it could do.

My dad had been so kind and gentle and so loving when he was around. He'd only ever shouted at me once or twice and I'd hated it when he had done so; it was all the worse for being rare. I never knew he'd been dealing with issues that weighed down on him. He was on anti-addiction pills to help him quit smoking and I know now that there's a strong correlation between them and suicide. One of his brothers, my namesake Stephen, had died a long time ago – a year and a half before I was born. This I already knew but Ken told me that his other brother, David had hanged himself two years prior. That must have sowed a seed. It wasn't a quick or easy decision and he hadn't taken it lightly. It was something he had thought through. As I turned the events over in my mind I could only conclude that maybe he'd felt it was too late for him to change his circumstances; he'd made all his mistakes and he'd got to a point in his life where he couldn't live with them any more and couldn't go back and change any of it. So he gave up.

I got the first of my many tattoos as a result of his death. It was on my left arm, a gravestone with the word 'Dad' as a way of permanently marking that moment. Now I wanted to do everything I could do to live positively. Next I stopped smoking weed. I was 24 and had been smoking properly for ten years but I didn't want to rely on weed as I was going through grieving. I wanted to feel everything that I had to feel, deal with the suicide and get through it without crutches. I did smoke one spliff on the day of the funeral and then, with very few exceptions, I have only smoked very occasionally since then.

It took a good few months of being weed-free to notice any positive changes, but once the smoke cleared I felt like I was seeing the world through different eyes. It put me on a different footing with friends who were still smoking heavily. I didn't make a conscious effort to cut off from those people but inevitably I spent less time with them. Distance had also been growing between me and most of Haunted House Productions. Alex and I had left to focus on music, which was quite often different to the tastes of the others. We had all stayed friends for a while but we were beginning to speak less. I knew something was wrong when Chyna didn't show up to the 'Upper Clapton Dance' video shoot. And these weren't the only factors in my deepening sense of isolation. There was also the fact that not all of my friends agreed with me dealing now that I wasn't just dealing weed. And quite apart from anything else, I just didn't see people so much. I was living in Woodford, away from a lot of my friends and I was struggling emotionally. My relationship with Tia also came to an end – temporarily at least, as we would have a reconciliation some 18 months later.

On the other hand, I was still writing songs. Out of that period of my life, for example, came 'Goodnight', which would end up closing my first album just over two years later. Some songs happen in minutes, but that one deals with the struggles I had after Edie's death. I finally finished it after my dad died, as if whatever feelings were released by his passing I was able to put into the music.

I continued to write with Alex. He produced a load of my tracks under his alias Cores and executive-produced the first three albums, as well as what now came out of our sessions, *The Green EP*. I felt easy experimenting in Alex's company and that made for better music. There shouldn't be any rights and wrongs in the way you write and neither of us were embarrassed by trying out ideas, even when it didn't work or we ended up down a dead end. I felt encouraged to develop by him, just as I have been by others in the studio such as Mike Skinner.

That said, the seven-track *The Green EP* was also a major fucking stress. We didn't have much time and, as easy as our relationship could be, in many respects Alex and I operated in completely opposite ways. I might get an idea for a new track while I'm working on something else and I'm quite happy to leave the other song where it is and go off in a different direction. As long as I keep interested and the creative juices are flowing, I'm satisfied, but Alex is very process-driven and when things get out of his control he gets freaked out.

The EP had been something we decided to do quickly to finance a tour with the Gym Class Heroes on which I'd been invited as support and it all came together in just four days. It was a tense time: I'd get into the zone late at night, jumping from track to track and Alex would be struggling to stay awake, then he'd flip out and we'd have to take a break while he cooled off. Somehow, our partnership worked, we got the tracks together and Ged got the EP pressed and released towards the end of 2008.

It was following the launch that I got a message from Adele. Even before I read it I knew what it was about. I also thought it meant trouble. Nutty P, a producer who was one of the many people I met at the Jump Off, had sent me a beat using a sample of Adele's 2007 song 'Hometown Glory'. Her single hadn't charted when it was first released but I loved it and it became the basis of my remix version on *The Green EP*. But I hadn't cleared the sample – I wasn't even in a proper record deal at the time – so when I opened up MySpace to see an inbox message from Adele my first thought was, Oh shit, I'm getting a cease-and-desist and I'm gonna have to remove it from MySpace and dump all the CDs we've just pressed. It was nothing of the sort and if I'd been a bit more in the swim of things, I might have realised that Adele's lawyers wouldn't be contacting me via

MySpace. Instead, it was from the lady herself and she had only written to say she liked what I'd done and thanked me for using her song.

I met Adele again, years later, and I was partly responsible for her getting soaked in beer. That was at an Example show in Shepherd's Bush. He'd reserved a row of seats on the balcony for his close friends and Adele was among them. It was a time when me and Example were both doing really well and a lot of his fans were fans of mine. As I walked in a few people recognised me, which led to everyone downstairs turning to look at the balcony to see what the fuss was about. A little cheer erupted, everyone got a bit excited and a guy behind us, probably not the sharpest pencil in the pot, got over-enthusiastic and threw his hands up in the air, chucking his pint over our whole row – including Adele. She took it well, but I'm sorry about that, Adele. I'd love to work with her (again) but given the level of success she's attained since then I don't think that's likely, even without the beer-soaking. I still love the 'Hometown Glory' remix – 'It's hard to flower in the shadow of a tower block' – one of the early ones that I really enjoy going back to every now and again.

The Green EP itself shifted just enough to take us out on the road although it didn't do amazingly well in terms of sales. I certainly didn't have much money, although many people assumed I was doing all right because of a big prize I won at the Jump Off earlier in the year for which MySpace put up £50,000. The money was to go to the overall battle rap winner that July and I faced tough competition. I was still a major target because of my previous win. I got to the final and faced up to Stig, a large northern guy and a notorious battle rapper. I was victorious with lines such as, 'He's so fat he gets out of breath just by breathing,' but received the prize money in the form of advertising space on MySpace rather than cash. Back then, MySpace was still a bigger social network than Facebook and so it was good for my profile – but it would still have been nicer if I could have spent it. On my teeth.

7. NOPE, I'M FUCKED

I got my 'Lucky' tattoo done on my neck by Demian Cervera as an ode to a more positive outlook and about two weeks later a total stranger tried to kill me, stabbing through the design and into my neck with a broken bottle.

I'd had a number of tattoos done since I marked my father's death with a gravestone. There was the skeletal professor, pictured among his chemical jars with smoke billowing out of them and smoking a spliff. That'll be a fun one to explain to the kids. Then I got 'PG' initialled on my neck. I guess that was my way of deciding it was really all or nothing with music: tattoos were not as common then and I knew that my decision to do above the shoulders wouldn't recommend me for any jobs in the normal world. These days things are changing. People are more accepting of tattoos, partly thanks to the influx of hipsters and their fucking beards.

Not all of the tattoos had significance. I had started with a very meaningful one in the form of my dad's memorial, but generally I got to thinking of my tattoos in the same way as I did with my songs. Some had a deep symbolism, some related to a place and time and others were just mindless fun, pure imagery that appealed to me. More recently I've had my fingers done, spelling 'care less' or 'careless' – both apply.

At the time of the Lucky tattoo I was still charging around London on my Yamaha R125 making deliveries. I couldn't quite yet call music my career again, but I had enough money to keep making music. Life wasn't terrible, in other words. The Lucky tattoo was done in May 2009 and appears as it was intended – without scarring, in other words – in the video for 'Upper Clapton Dance', the song that was later re-released as a bonus track on my second album.

I was trying hard to live up to my resolution to live more positively when I was attacked. On a night out with my friends Anthony and Haydon, I ended up at Cargo, the nightclub in Shoreditch, London. I bumped into old friends and, with DJ EZ spinning old-school garage we were getting quite nostalgic and feeling like teenagers again.

The club was very busy. I was polite as I moved through the crowd but one bloke didn't hear me approach. I said, 'Excuse me', a second time as I squeezed through, gently putting my hand on the guy's back so he was aware I was there and so I wasn't just pushing past. As I walked on someone shouted, 'Oi!' but it didn't really register as the voice wasn't familiar. I heard another 'Oi!', turned around and realised it was the two men I'd just passed.

'You barged my mate.' I was confused. He wasn't even the one I had touched. He told me to shake his friend's hand and say, 'Sorry'. I'd had a few drinks and I wasn't in the mood for following instructions. Because of the racket he was making, we were getting ourselves an audience. I was annoyed at being told what to do. I don't consider myself to be 'hard', whatever people might think of rappers, tattoos and the rest. I've always been aware of being tall but I've have never thrown my weight around. There had been nothing antagonising or rude in how I moved past the two of them and I knew I was in the right.

The guy continued. 'You think you're a badman? You think you're the baddest man in here?' He got right in my face as he did so, his nose briefly touching mine. I'm not a big fan of space invaders.

'I ain't a bad man but I'm not a pussy,' I said. I grabbed the back of his collar, nutted him just hard enough to let him know what I was on and pushed him away. He backed down, muttering, 'Cool, cool, cool.'

That was that, then. Or so I thought. Everyone stopped staring and began to talk again. Haydon came over and suggested we leave, but I wasn't leaving because of a stupid and pointless drunken argument. But five minutes later the man who had been arguing with me came at me from behind. I heard a noise, someone saying, 'He's got something in his hand.' I turned around to see a flash of his hand rising fast towards my face. I lifted my arm, attempting to deflect him, but he stabbed me with a jagged half-bottle. It pierced the left side of my neck, straight through the 'Lucky' tattoo. I lifted my hand and I felt the warmth of the blood pissing out through my fingers, spilling on to the floor. I screamed and began to try and escape the club. It made no sense. How had this gone from a few words to someone trying to kill me? All I'd hurt was his feelings. It was sheer cowardice. All the time the blood continued to pour.

They say that when you're stabbed for a moment you don't realise what's happened – not true in my case. I knew straight away. No pain – that would come later, after the adrenaline and the shock wore off – but I was in no doubt that I was in a fight for my life. I managed to make my way through the crowded club and out of the doors. I began to feel weak on my feet, so I took a seat on the kerb. As I did, I got hit over the back of the head. The bloke who stabbed me had followed me out. I turned and grabbed him, still trying to hold my neck together, while he shouted, 'You're dead... you're fucking dead!' as we rolled about on the floor. We were split up by passing police who rushed to the scene. Panic was clearly visible on the faces of the strangers around me but I found myself in a weird state of calm.

My phone had gone flying but someone handed it back and I called my nan and then my mum to apologise. I felt somehow responsible and disappointed in myself for allowing it to happen. 'I'm really sorry,' I said. 'I love you. I'm really, really sorry, but I don't know if I'll ever see you again.' I could feel my life bleeding out of me as I waited for the ambulance to arrive. It seemed to take an eternity.

At A&E they said it was almost impossible there was any damage to major arteries – I'd have been dead already if so – but nevertheless the wound was severe and located in a part of the neck packed with complicated mechanics. They would need to carry out a delicate surgical procedure. I briefly saw Anthony when he arrived at hospital. He'd jumped straight in when I got stabbed and also been smacked round the face with a bottle that had broken his nose. I felt worse for him than I did for myself as whoever bottled him had done a right job on his nose. But then I hadn't seen my neck at that point and everyone had tried to reassure me that it wasn't that bad. Lying fuckers.

Before I went down for the op, I just had time to be spoken to by the police. They arrested me. Upon going through my clothes and items on my person they found something in one of my pockets. And then I was under. The surgery itself was expected to take an hour but the wound turned out to be deeper than they first thought and I ended up on the operating table for three and a half hours. The surgeons found the bottle had sliced through my salivary gland and only my jaw bone stopped it tearing right through my throat. The first thing the surgeon asked me to do when I came round was shrug my shoulders. I found that odd until they said they'd made a nerve twitch during surgery that could have cost me the use of my arms. No shrugging matter, then. I came around to find my mum and my nan – together for the first time in years. Ged was there, as well as my sister – my mum's daughter – and I was nice to her. 'Thanks for coming,' I said before passing out again. I came back round to see everyone else, I thanked them again for coming then followed up with, 'Now please can you all fuck off.' Or at least, that's what they later told me I said. I was so fucked on the anaesthetic I don't remember a thing.

I didn't respond well to the anaesthetic and alongside sickness and dizziness I got hiccups. Fucking hiccups. Imagine having 38 external stitches, god knows how many internal stitches, a massively painful and swollen neck… and hiccups. Now imagine having them for 48 hours. I tried everything I could to get rid of them and by the time they stopped I felt like I'd strained every bloody muscle in my diaphragm.

When I was conscious enough to properly process

information, the doctor explained that the bottle had passed the carotid artery that runs right through the body. If the bottle had got the carotid, I would have bled out in four minutes and that would have been that. But the doctor assured me I was going to make a full recovery and I had more visitors in the form of Hattie Collins and Chantelle Fiddy from *RWD* magazine. They were friends since early on in my career and had been at Cargo the night before. They brought me a phone charger and a fake chain, putting a smile on my face. A lot of other people followed, including Ara and Harry from Jump Off, who came over with BBC hip-hop DJ Charlie Sloth. Everyone was in shock because, despite the introduction of Form 696 – the risk-assessment document for club nights required by police – and the odd report in the papers, violence is not a regular part of urban nights.

After I was discharged I returned to my mum's to recuperate. She lived in Leytonstone by the Cathall estate. But I really wanted to give the relationship a chance and I hoped that living under her roof would bring us together. I began the healing process, thinking about what had happened. I was in shock to begin with and it was only with time that I realised how close I had come to dying. That knowledge left me feeling very, very low. In my head I knew how fortunate I was but I just didn't feel that I was lucky. Yet that same evening a 16-year-old was stabbed in the neck not ten minutes from Cargo, on Amhurst Road in Hackney and died from his injuries. I had survived, a good thing that nevertheless just seemed to highlight an awful lot of what was wrong in my life.

What did I have to look forward to? I was stuck in my mum's house with a huge bandage and a scar I'd have to see every time I caught my reflection. I'd achieved a bit of notoriety in the music scene but I wasn't making headway with my music. Some people might want to brag about their misfortunes and show their war wounds with pride but I didn't look at it like that. I had been a hair's breadth away from death, a disastrous fucking waste. What had happened had both shocked and scared me and I couldn't allow myself to be scared and so the fear turned into anger. After the anger came a crash. Depression.

Depression had been a consistent presence in my life but this time I was more than bogged down. I had friends who cared and tried to cheer me up, but everything I'd achieved seemed to be in the past. What could I do? I felt I was too old to go back into education and that I was a total failure. I didn't talk about how bad I felt to anyone, I isolated the emotions and bottled them up. I made out like it was minor – I'd say, 'Shit happens, innit, I'm hardly the only person ever to get stabbed,' and tried not to show how badly I was feeling inside.

The Sun sent a reporter round to my mum's to speak to me because knife crime was then a live issue and they wanted to write something on the debate over whether clubs should be serving drinks in glasses. The obvious answer being, 'Yes', because things taste better in a glass and we live in a civilised fucking society. I talked with the reporter and he took my picture, only for me to get a call from them later saying they were sorry but they'd pulled the story because Katie Price had fallen through a glass table and cut her leg and the stories were too similar. How was a celebrity leg wound similar to an attack that almost resulted in a death? The kind of violence that is all too commonplace and needs to be highlighted and dealt with? But people need their celebrity fix and a celebrity I was not. That non-story was the first time a tabloid took any interest in me and it was my introduction to the surreal and illogical world of showbiz reporting.

It was two weeks before I went out again. In the meantime, I went over the night at Cargo in my mind. Maybe I should have known better than to aggravate the situation? But part of me still believed I was right to stand up for myself. The other part wondered if it was ever really worth it. Pride had definitely played a part in my response. The guy was drunk and aggressive: for the sake of a bit of peace would it really have hurt me to laugh, say, 'All right, mate, whatever, cool,' shake his hand and carried on with my evening?

That first night out after the attack coincided with Skream's birthday. I had met the dubstep producer a couple of months earlier at the Miami Winter Music Conference when I had jetlag and couldn't sleep. I'd been up and working on what would end up as the chorus for 'I Need You Tonight' and I was restless. We bonded over Superman alcoholic slush puppies in South Beach that contained 191-proof vodka. We nailed four of them, a new record. Now, back in the UK, we were out on what would once have been just one of many very ordinary nights. But heading back to a club after what had happened I was hyper-aware of everything going on around me – and that feeling has always returned when I've been clubbing since.

I eased into the evening, it felt cool to be among friends. Our group included Plastician, who'd first introduced me to Skream and Skream's brother HiJak. I left at about five in the morning and went back to mine with the girl I was seeing at the time. When I woke it was not yet 11 o'clock, which puzzled me. I normally wouldn't have risen from my pit until 2 or 3 pm and I felt as though I'd dodged a hangover – for about ten minutes. Then the vomiting began. Two hours later

I was still going, retching and heaving the nothing that was left in my stomach.

Normally I was pretty careful about my health but Mum had to drag me against my will to the doctor. There was no sympathy to be had: I was told my tolerance to alcohol had become non-existent while recovering from the attack and the codeine (that I enjoyed until the constipation became a problem) had completely shot my stomach lining. The doctor drew me a nice little graph that showed the way in which my body dealt with alcohol and, more importantly, the point at which it stopped dealing with alcohol. And then he drew a massive spike – where people died. I'd given myself proper alcohol poisoning. A second near-death experience in as many weeks. Blinding night out though.

Skream's name came up again when I got a Facebook message from Lily Allen. I had been out running errands and had just shot home to grab a couple more bits. As I did so I checked my account and noticed Lily had contacted me from Stockholm where she said she'd seen Skream and another musician named Benga. I jokingly told her to watch out because Skream was a proper liability. He was one of a few friends that I shared with Lily. I didn't know her so well at that point – I'd only seen her out a couple of times and we had been introduced by a guy who played both in her band and previously with Mike Skinner. But it wasn't until Crispin Somerville, who would later run her record label, played her 'I Need You Tonight', that she decided to get in touch with me via social media.

We talked generally about the music we were each doing and I mentioned I'd cleared rights for 'Dub Be Good To Me' by Beats International. That turned out to be a favourite song of hers and she asked to hear my version. I sent it over and she immediately suggested that she sing the hook and invited me to perform it with her on stage at Bestival in September.

Right place, right time. If I hadn't caught that message at that time Lily's performance on what became 'Just be Good to Green' might never have happened. But now I was under a deadline with just a few weeks to go before the festival. We had to get the song done quickly. The night before we were to record together, Lily was out with Skream and Benga when she fell backwards off the stage behind the DJ booth and did her back in.

We eventually made it to the studio and there was an initial awkwardness since we hadn't hung out much before, but it didn't last long. I enjoyed being back in the studio – a welcome change from making deliveries on my bike – and here I was making my return by recording with one of the biggest artists in the country. I was a little bit tentative and wary during that session. I think we were both nervous in our own ways. As she was leaving the studio, Lily casually asked, 'Have you got any tours booked or anything?' When I said I hadn't, she said, 'Why don't you come on tour with me?' All I could think was, is she serious? And she was.

Bestival soon came around and I headed over to the Isle of Wight to prepare for the gig. My manager, Ged, is well-seasoned when it comes to festivals. He didn't stay on site, instead booking a little cottage nearby – sadly, there were no bedrooms going spare and only armchairs in the living room. I ended up crashing in a sleeping bag under the kitchen table. A rarely followed rule of attending festivals is resolving not to go too hard the first night. For artists, that usually translates to reining it in until after the performance. But I arrived on the Thursday and our slot wasn't until Saturday. It wasn't only my first show with Lily but also my first real show for a long time and I was nervous but also determined to get it right. I vowed to keep it civilised. By sun-up on Friday I hadn't had much sleep.

Everyone else arrived later on Friday – including Lily and Skream – and, though I was worried that I'd burnt all my matches, it turned out that I still had a few in the box. Lily retired at a reasonable time but Skream and a few of us carried on back at the cottage and, as the sun came up, Skream and I polished off – and this memory is distinct – a large vodka with Marks & Spencer pomegranate juice. Then we jumped in a taxi back to the site, found everyone else and pretty much carried on where we'd left off.

Somehow it was suddenly the afternoon and I found myself standing in the wings of the main stage, although Lily's security man, Trevor, didn't want to let me near her and was manoeuvring to put his hands on me as I walked up. She had to tell him, 'No, no, it's fine, this is Stephen, Professor Green.' Given that I'd been up for 24 hours I can understand him being somewhat wary, but we got on well and he would later end up doing security for me too. As I waited to go on, Skream asked: 'Are you nervous?'

I replied 'Nope, I'm fucked!' with a stupid grin on my face and walked out on stage. I'm often anxious for all kinds of reasons but I rarely get stage-fright. Battling set me up well for doing gigs: each is a different craft and each presents its own challenges but the spontaneity involved with battling made it more unpredictable and gave me much more to be nervous about than gigging.

Lily and I hadn't rehearsed at all but I knew the song inside out. There were 30,000 or more people looking at us

– ultimately, all I had to do was remember my words. And not fall off the stage (which I had once done during one of my few losses at Jump Off). I walked out in glorious sunshine to Lily dressed up as an alien – a hot alien. Barely anybody knew who I was. I can't say that at that point I thought I'd ever be attracting similarly sized crowds myself, not to mention returning to Bestival in my own right a year later. But I knew it was a good start. I left the stage and the Isle of Wight pleased with how things were going.

While my music was building again I had decided to make another go of the relationship with Tia. But this second – and final – attempt would also be ultimately unsuccessful. I became really uncomfortable about the idea that people might pry into our relationship as I started to pick up momentum – and later tabloid attention. I didn't even want people to know who my girlfriend was; I didn't want people in my business like that. If I had been more honest with myself I would have seen that there was so much change in my life that relationships were too much for me to deal with.

Tia found it hard to come to terms with my attitude and when things came to a head it was because she felt that I wanted to pretend I didn't have a girlfriend. That hadn't been my idea at all, but we worked ourselves up into one of those final sorts of arguments – she started to say something and stopped but I managed to prise it out of her. I already knew what she was about to say. She said, 'Sometimes I just wish that it had never happened.' She was talking about my career taking off. That was the end. There could be nothing for us after that.

Lily's tour – It's Not Me, It's You – had been running since March and after Bestival was to make its way through mainland Europe, the UK and then Australia into the new year. In the run-up to going away I had to make one special arrangement. I was living with my friend Anthony – the one who'd jumped in when I was stabbed – another old friend called Martin and one other guy in Chingford, east London and with me not around I needed someone to take care not only of my beloved staffie Alfie but also a new pup I'd got called Tiny. Alfie – now fully grown and trained – needed less attention and so stayed at my nan's, but it proved hard to find someone who could look after and give Tiny the attention he needed while I was away. Helpfully, though, my mum recommended a friend. The woman loved dogs, she told me, she'd be more than happy to help out. I was doubtful as I didn't know this friend at all but my mum vouched for her and said it would be fine. So I took Tiny over, said a fond goodbye and with that I was all set to go on tour.

Nobody in the audiences we played to had a clue about me apart from the tiny handful of people at each venue who knew me from my Beats days or from battling. To the vast majority of Lily's crowd I was some guy, wheeled on for a song or two who disappeared again. But that began to change, slowly, as we crossed countries. I noticed that more people would sing along with 'Just Be Good to Green'. At first it was just the chorus, familiar to anyone who knew the SOS Band or the Beats International version. But later in the tour, some fans began to rap along to the verses too. It was a welcome progression.

The tour coincided with one of the most anxious periods of my life. Anxiety had been a part of me since I was a child. When I was little it had settled in my stomach and it periodically bubbled to the surface throughout my life. I've always needed to find a reason for it and where there was no reason I would invariably create one – often connected to my health. I'd feel a physical symptom – like the knots in my stomach that I sensed as a child – or, now I was older, a more abstract worry about the possibility of something being wrong with my health. I later went over the anxiety with a therapist and that was when I came to realise that my worry manifests itself as a result of stress. When I'm under a great deal of stress, I become almost manic and I fixate on what can just be theoretical risks. I've ended up having more tests than you can shake a stick at. It's just one of the many things related to depression and anxiety that I have had to fight over the years.

On the road my fears found their focus in the risks of casual sex – and there were plenty of opportunities for that as I went out on tour. So I started feeling sickly and when my glands went up after I bumped uglies with a bird in Germany so did my worry levels. But there were no doctors available as it was a weekend. I had to wait until I had a few days off before the UK tour started. I had no real reason to be concerned about anything relating to my brief German encounter as I was always far too careful. My paranoia around health didn't allow for any protection slip-ups – or slip-offs – but a consultation with Dr Google brought up the inevitably horrific array of suggestions. Despite many less severe suggestions, it was the worst of the bunch that stood out.

Chris Benns was a good friend through all of this craziness. He was a completely trustworthy mate and he helped me to manage my fears and organise things. I went to a private GP – one I would go on to see so many times that he ended up on the guest list at my wedding. (Big up Dr Malik.) I gave the doctor a full account and he told me I had nothing to worry about, but said that if it would put my mind at ease he'd test for everything. Great, I thought. But the catch was I had to wait four weeks before having the tests to ensure they were accurate.

Four weeks inched by with my mind flipping around, knowing I was being ridiculous and yet being extremely worried. Finally, the test results came back clear, which occasioned a big sigh of relief. But then one of my housemates mentioned that he'd had the exact same thing a few days before I arrived home. It had just been a virus/stomach bug going around. (Cheers, bro! Really, Anthony – thank you! Could have done with that info a touch sooner…)

With the tour finished I looked forward to seeing my dogs again and settling back home. One of my first jobs was ringing the number I had for my mum's dog-sitting friend and her boyfriend. No answer. Eventually her fella responded to say Tiny was at his brother's house. That sparked a sense that something was wrong straight away. It transpired that this woman was a 'recovered' heroin addict and her boyfriend had just come out of jail… not ideal candidates when looking for a pet-sitter. I went to his place ready for whatever might happen but just ended up banging on their door with no answer. I was walking back to my bike when I saw the woman and her boyfriend down the road. They saw me too and ran. I never caught up with them.

It was my mum I was angry with, more than with anyone else. She had vouched for someone she didn't properly know and when I confronted her about it she just gave me excuses and blamed other people for giving her reassurances. And then she said, 'Well, we both have to take responsibility for this.' I was furious.

'All I'm responsible for is trusting you,' I said.

At the time I wanted to cut off communication with her for

good – as it was, it would be years before we spoke again and even now we're still only at the start of working through things. Her attitude when I'd lost my dog had been the final straw as far as I was concerned. I'd been forced into a situation that could have jeopardised my future just at a point when things were going so well – it was a good thing I didn't catch them when they ran off. Had she just said, 'Sorry, I can't help,' in the first place I'd have made other arrangements. But I'd put my faith in her and she'd let me down. Mum can be quite negative – understandable with some of the challenges she's faced – but with this coming after a few other even more severe incidents I decided I needed some space from her. I was at a happy place in my life and I didn't want that to change.

There was at least a happy ending to one part of this story. I'd had Tiny microchipped and two years later I got a phone call from a vet who had identified me as the owner. Through talking to the doctor that Tiny had been left with, I pieced together what had happened. The boyfriend of the woman had sold Tiny to his dealer – or rather had exchanged my little puppy for some skag. Tiny was kept by the dealer until he got himself arrested. The dealer had visited his doctor who he knew to be a dog lover and told her he was certain he was going to jail. He made no mention of Tiny but when she left work she found Tiny tied to her car. Tiny wasn't all that tiny by this point and despite making progress with him and her own dogs she knew she wasn't going to be able to keep him. So she'd taken him to her vet who found the chip.

I was over the moon, but also worried that Tiny might have been mistreated and used for his size, making him aggressive in order to intimidate people and look after the dealer. I drove to pick up Tiny and when he saw me he was beside himself.

When the door opened he just ran around in circles pissing all over my feet – what a greeting. He'd been taken very good care of and he'd turned into a very good, very big dog. Too big and too grown, unfortunately, to learn to get on with Alfie. Tom Norey, one of my best mates in Woodford, and his girlfriend Holly have him now. Tom now runs a dog-walking business and kennels – if only he'd had the idea earlier. Tiny's big and fat and spoilt rotten and he's as happy as Larry. And I still get to see him when I'm in the area visiting Nan.

My mum was definitely cut out of my life and my decision to do that was part of the more focused attitude I was adopting in everything I did. I was cutting out the difficult parts of my life and for a while that worked. I knocked the dealing on the head for the second and final time (fingers crossed). I'd spent too long straddling two worlds and I was determined, when I saw those first glimmers of making my hobby my career again, to leave everything behind that would distract me from the music.

Having Lil on board definitely helped to move things along. Once she recorded 'Just Be Good to Green' and with the winter's touring confirmed, there was more excitement around me than ever before. The music industry was opening its doors to me once more. A guy called Harry Lloyd-Jones from Virgin called to ask for a meeting – Virgin being one of those that had turned me down after The Beats – and Ged gave him an ultimatum: 'Fine,' he said, 'we'll come in, but if we do there's got to be a deal on the table.' Harry committed to it on the phone there and then, and he was as good as his word. It was Harry and Virgin who said, 'Let's fucking do it.'

8. I CAN'T HANDLE MY DRUGS

I'm not a fan of champagne in general but when I signed with Virgin a few corks were popped. Well, it's traditional when you sign away your freedom.

After months of little interest it was quite odd how quickly things changed, but what had changed? The answer seemed to be Lily but maybe it was also that I had almost died as the result of a stab wound. The industry had been waiting for one more thing to happen, one more piece of the puzzle to fall into place. I remember being raided and arrested in Euston at a time when I was winding everything down and about to sign with Mike's label. If anything had landed in my lap I might have been looking at a short bird. When I told Mike I thought he'd be disappointed but actually all he said was, 'Everyone's got a story – at least yours is interesting.' I guess that was even more true after the twists and turns that 2009 had thrown at me. With Tim Vigon having helped get my music back from Warner I had some tracks for the album, but there was still work to be done.

I got straight down to it. We recorded a lot of the album at Alex's, hardly the glamorous setting you might expect after getting a major label deal. Nothing much had changed. As I had done in the past, I would stand in his wardrobe to record my vocals while he sat in his living room at his desk. It was DIY but Alex was an amazingly skilled producer. We again had very different approaches to recording – I'd be very loose and jump around from track to track and he'd be pulling in the opposite direction, meticulous and focused on getting the album together. Weirdly, I suppose that, combined, we're quite a balanced human or we would be if we weren't two different people.

As ever, it was confidence that was important for working in the studio and for trying out new material. When I'm not feeling confident or if I'm uncomfortable about running the risk of sounding stupid, then I know I'm going to limit myself. A lot of my music has been written while pacing and saying things out loud, anything, just waiting for something magic to come out – and there have been times when I haven't felt at ease, haven't felt myself and I've left the studio after an entire day with absolutely nothing. When I leave with nothing at all I find there's a knock-on effect. I can easily start beating myself up the next day, just as I'm heading into a new session. It's as if my anxiety develops a voice in my head. 'What if I can't write anything again today? What if this is it? What if I have nothing left to say?' A voice better off ignored.

The first session I did towards the album after signing was set up by Sam Evitt from Virgin (who has since gone on to huge things and now manages Sam Smith and Disclosure, among others) and Harry Lloyd-Jones, my A&R. I got to work with people I hadn't previously known, starting with a musician and producer who worked out of Ealing Studios – Shahid Khan, aka Naughty Boy. I'm always polite when I meet people and I don't have any trouble making convo but the session was an artificial situation. It doesn't always work. Putting two artists in a room isn't an exact science; however talented each other may be, you can't always guarantee the right chemistry needed to make good music. You can't force something like that. But as it was, we immediately bonded. Naughty Boy had some AK-47, I hadn't smoked weed in a long time and together we banged out the whole of 'Kids That Love to Dance' there and then (have a listen to the first line, it's all there – 'I can't handle my drugs, so blame Shah and his handful of buds').

Naughty Boy was incredible with ideas and quite unorthodox in how he worked. I firmly believed he was a fucking evil genius – he's even got a cat like Ernst Blofeld – except that he wasn't evil in the slightest. He has one of the kindest hearts of anyone I've met. Through him I met Sunny and the Mojam production duo (Mus Omer and James Murray, formerly Strider and Flava of Blazin' Squad glory), who also worked on the album. Between them, the three are responsible for more of my productions than anyone else.

That first day Naughty Boy had himself brought along someone else for me to work with, a singer who sat quietly on the sidelines and seemed very unassuming while me and Shah were just sat there being stoned. The track was still untitled at this stage but I'd done most of my lyrics – I freestyled most of what came out, it would just happen like that back then. This singer chilled, listening to what we were working through for the verses, before at last saying, 'I think I've got something, guys.' She went into the booth without having sung her part and in one take recorded it. And it was perfect. That was that. Done. No re-recording needed. 'Kids That Love to Dance' was both the obvious album opener and and my introduction to Emeli Sandé, the singer I've since worked with more than any other.

Emeli pops up with me on tracks that people may not even know about – and as I got to know her much better I have found that she's not generally the unassuming quiet type. I think of her as a real artist in the songwriting sense because, despite everything I've done, I sometimes struggle to think of myself as a 'proper' songwriter. Maybe that's because I wasn't trained for it but around her it doesn't matter. I've never felt my approach to be a problem and I'm always totally comfortable working with Emeli. I'm always happy to send her lines I'd like her to sing or to help me develop. I'm lucky to have her at the end of the phone. She's inspired and brought to life some of my favourite tracks.

The session format hasn't always worked out as well as it did that first day. I've done studio work with producers and singers that have gone nowhere at all. At first I would worry and not quite understand why I was having problems coming up with material. I've come to realise that sometimes it just doesn't work and there's no real reason behind it. But a lot of my music has ended up being recorded in that studio in Ealing – F Block, part of the Ealing film studios complex.

There were four floors, with Naughty Boy's studio on the ground floor and Sunny working further up, with Mojam above him. When I met Mojam one of the first things they said was that we both had a mutual friend. They gave me a name and I agreed I did know it – it was my link Dave. They reminded me that I'd sold the brother of someone they knew a kilo back in my shotting days. And I did recall loading the brother's blue plumber van in Holloway Road. Another collision of my two worlds.

I have never been a singer myself and on that first album I certainly hadn't expected to have to do any singing. I wouldn't have done had it just been me there, but I'm always open to working in different ways and it was Fink who pushed me into doing it when we worked together. We both featured on 'Closing the Door', the first of our collaborations, which we wrote together. He also produced it.

I don't play any instruments (still on the to-do list) but I always work closely with producers on ideas and shaping the beats and I'd write a lot of the vocals for people to sing on my tracks, melodies too. My view is that you might be able to learn to play an instrument but you can't really be taught how to be creative. Mike Skinner had suggested that I read his music theory books but I think creativity is innate and I'm glad I haven't let ideas in books shape me.

Not everything I'd hoped for made it to the final cut. The Stone Roses' Ian Brown was meant to do a song. Ged put me in touch with him because he thought we'd get on well and Ian responded to me directly. We got on well, although in the back of my mind I was always feeling slightly amazed that I was in touch with the singer from such an influential band, without which we might not have had Oasis. The track I had planned for him featured an ELO sample and he was, like, 'I'm not doing anything with those Brummies.' I completely reworked the track, dropping the ELO sample, but then things in his life took over and it never came about.

I kept on performing live alongside working in the studio and racked up the miles trying to keep up with the competing demands. Once I had a gig lined up in Cardiff with another the following night in Bristol. It could have been a sensible schedule over a couple of days as the two cities are only about half an hour away from each other but work on the album was too urgent to take any time out. I had to get off stage in Cardiff and drive all the way back to London at stupid o'clock in the morning – passing Bristol on the way – so I could get to work on the album with Mojam. I wrote 'Monster' on the way to the studio the next day after far too little sleep and then recorded that song, along with 'City of Gold'. No break: I got straight back in the car – a rented Vauxhall Astra with Chris Benns at the wheel – and went to Bristol.

Another time we did London to Middlesbrough and back in the same night, getting backache in the same Vauxhall Astra. Chris was with me all the way. He had been doing steadily more work, including tour managing and he came with me on those late night runs to make sure the PAs ran smoothly.

But it wasn't all motorway commuting. Having done the dates with Lily, we stayed in touch and at one point she dropped a conversational bomb in that ever-so-casual fashion of hers. We'd barely finished the final Brixton show, having a drink in her dressing room when she says 'Greeners, I want you to come to Australia with me.' Her agent (who was now also looking after me) Alex Nightingale was in earshot and for him this was panic-inducing. The Australian tour was in January 2010 and with Christmas coming up I didn't have long to get a work visa. But I've always thought chances are generally presented to be taken – life doesn't always hand you aces so when it does... why not? And so one of the first things I did with my advance from Virgin was buy a ticket to Australia.

We got all the paperwork done in time while I fulfilled some commitments with the label and did some more work on the album. I was then sharing a flat in Bow, east London, with my friend Jack Cannon and from London I flew out to meet Lily mid-tour. I'd love to say I landed and couldn't believe I was in Australia but I could; it definitely felt like I'd travelled halfway round the world.

The trip opened up even more opportunities and introduced me to some amazing people. I bumped into Dizzee, met the Kasabian guys and Lil brought me along on a day trip with Muse on an absolutely ridiculous four-tier yacht. The night after the first gig I was hanging with Johnny Drum Machine and his bro Eddie who I'd known since the street days. Johnny knew Dom from Muse and so we went for a drink in his room – leaving after emptying the mini-bar. Back on the yacht, after some time spent lying on deck and looking up at the mast, the three of us eventually plucked up the courage to climb right up to the top and jump off. We didn't know we were having a swim with ocean predators – no one told me about the sharks in Sydney Harbour. I'm just glad I returned to the boat with all of my limbs.

Another only slightly less dangerous stunt I did down under was to send my ex-girlfriend Naoko a pissed text. That had been quite a step, in that I hadn't spoken to her in years, not since we had the argument when I started seeing Tia. But Naoko got back to me and we eventually re-established contact. It took a while before we felt like real friends again. At first it was all very brittle; so much time had passed and so much had happened. At one point she responded to a disagreement we had by accusing me of saying something only because I was famous. I retorted that it was because she was being a fucking idiot at that particular moment. That broke the awkwardness and we've stayed close friends ever since.

Back in the UK I found that the trusty bike I'd been getting about on had been stolen – I wasn't even the tiniest bit pissed off, to be honest, I took it as a sign – and got my own Addison Lee account. Everything felt better, I was busy enough to stop my thoughts from becoming anxious ones and I was working on something I loved. I had a lot of people willing me on as well. Chantelle and Hattie, Paul H from *Hip-Hop Connection*, DJ Semtex, MistaJam, Shortee Blitz, Ara and Harry from the Jump Off, Zane Lowe, Manny Norté and Jez Welham; they were all behind me and many others were too. I was one of the first from my world to crossover to a major. And there were a lot of people who had shared the good and bad times during the journey. They'd helped me along my way, championed me and now they wanted to see me win. No doubt that played a huge part in it actually happening. The vibe was amazing. People showed me untold kindness and I was proper lucky for that.

In April 2010 'I Need You Tonight' was released as the lead single. I'd been planning to launch it with the Green Party, but the original venue was cancelled by the police. By their twisted logic I was some kind of dangerous person because I'd been involved in a stabbing – even though it was me that got stabbed. I got slapped by a Form 696 – convoluted risk-assessment paperwork – that killed my plans. We ended up in a notoriously scuzzy venue in Hoxton called the Macbeth. I asked my old friend Lewis, who's a food aficionado, to find us somewhere we could have a meal and 30 of us ended up piling into the basement room of a Vietnamese restaurant around the corner. It seemed a decent way to celebrate. Not for Cores though, he ordered a Chicken Royale – I mean, you wouldn't go to Burger King for Vietnamese would you?

Within a week I was in the charts. Even the label was surprised by the record's success, though we did have a pretty strong run-up. 'I Need You Tonight' actually outsold and charted higher than 'Just be Good to Green' with Lil, the follow-up in June. There'd been loose talk about the UK No 1 spot for 'I Need You Tonight', but I don't think anyone really expected that – I definitely didn't. It peaked at UK No 3, was record of the week on Radio 1 and received support from Capital and just about everywhere else. I'd had no expectations for its performance which made it quite easy to deal with. Anything was progress as far as I was concerned.

I didn't feel any different for being in the charts. If anything, I think about it more now; at the time it was something that was hard to digest when I was caught up in the moment. I would try to find time to reflect then but life was moving quickly and I was working as hard as I possibly could, scared of any break in momentum. Before I knew it, I was past that milestone, although I've definitely thought of some 'What the fuck?' moments while reminiscing: I started frequenting artisan coffee shops and quickly became a member of the notorious Groucho Club in Soho – I was the cunt I had never wanted to be. (I actually don't think being a member of the Groucho makes me a cunt – but my mate Aidan, aka Scribbler, who did the cover for this book, thinks me not thinking that definitely makes me a cunt.)

Some people said I had sold out by becoming a commercial artist but it wasn't a line of reasoning that made sense to me. I'd had 'I Need You Tonight' and 'Just Be Good To Green' as songs well before I joined Virgin. It wasn't as if I set out to change direction – there had always been two sides to my music as a songwriter. That version of Adele's 'Hometown Glory' on the *The Green EP* was one side to me that had always been there – I always had a desire to go for the big hook on a tune where I saw fit, but alongside that I've always made more straight-up rap tunes. I don't ever go into the studio with preconceptions about what I'm about to create: ideas present themselves and some lend themselves to one style over another. Some songs start as a street track and far exceed all expectations.

My music actually hasn't changed all that much over the years: 'Nothing More' is an early 'Read All About It' from *At Your Inconvenience*, 'Upper Clapton Dance' from *Lecture #1* has a similar vibe to 'Jungle' from *Alive Till I'm Dead* and 'Stereotypical Man' (also *Lecture #1*) is in a similar vein to 'I Need You Tonight'.

But people hear what they want to. It sometimes seemed as if half the world was going, 'Mate, you need to make another "Jungle", you've sold out.' And the other half would be listening to 'Hugs and Kisses' off *At Your Inconvenience* and saying, 'I don't want this hardcore shit, I like pop music.' And I can write about all of this and still there will be no fixed way of dictating what becomes a pop (-ular) song. Me? I was fine being in the charts. *Alive Till I'm Dead* came out in July and went straight in at its peak of UK No 2.

What followed that was a lot of hard graft to promote the album, although to be honest being a musician often didn't feel like work at all. Touring was still mainly fun and only occasionally terrifying, but even as a moderately successful artist it was sometimes tough to keep the pace up. When I did my first headline tour later in 2010 it got even more crazy. It wouldn't be unusual to be in central London for 6 am for an early TV slot (perhaps with my good pal and occasional rap spar Bill Turnbull) and then head straight to Manchester to set up, soundcheck, perform and drive home, with a similar schedule the next day. Or three PAs in one night, in two or three different towns. I would spend hours in a people carrier and, later, a Mercedes SUV, sharing the delights of travel with a rotating cast – over the years including Chris Benns, Felix, Jonah, Chyna, Alpha, Shereen, Trevor, Rufus, DJ IQ, Daryl and Haydon on the Gym Class Heroes tour, Lewis, Cores, Dream Mclean, Scribbler, Trevor, Katie and Thomas Jules. We've spent a lot of money on late-night Burger Kings at motorway service stations. Toddington, on the M1, is one of our favourites. We know it well. I didn't choose this life, this life chose me.

So I was working my backside off but I was flying high, no doubt about it, and was lucky enough to be based in a bachelor pad in Clerkenwell thanks to Luke, the friend I'd met through Naoko. Luke was off to Australia, didn't know how long he would be away and had got me in as a housesitter. His studio flat had high ceilings and a separate kitchen, although I don't think I ever cooked there once. It was perfect for all the mischief I wanted to get up to as a single man. Even if it was on a council estate. You'd think after all of those years living in council accommodation I'd have wanted to leave, but here I was on my own in another – very nice – council place.

I was enjoying the maelstrom of gigs, promo, partying, the lot, and it was a kick in the stomach to realise that I was barely breaking even. This was because of the deal I'd done with my publisher Bucks' sister company after leaving The Beats. Despite bringing it to everyone's attention, I hadn't got out of the deal before I signed with Virgin. Everyone – including the people at Bucks – were overjoyed with what was going on – why wouldn't they be? In all this excitement this 'small' matter was overlooked until I called Ged and said I was on my way to Bucks to sort things out myself. All of a sudden things got sorted pretty quickly but not without losing me pretty much everything I was working for. Sometimes a pound actually cost 10p to earn. It took a lot of time and money to get out of that situation; there was no Rolex sweeping for me for a while.

If you wanted to know how I was doing, the lyrics on many of the songs on the album gave a truer picture of where I was than you would imagine from my first taste of mainstream chart success that year. You might not realise from listening that I'm more often than not round my mate's house rapping in a dark cupboard, but you can tell from what the songs are about that my life hasn't really changed. I didn't have any cash to splash – or at least, not much. It wasn't like I was broke – despite the palaver, I was making money that equalled my former business. I could pay my rent, go out and eat, that kind of thing – but life definitely continued to be more Casio than Rolex for a while. With the – big – exception of a very generous and unexpected present from Lily.

I was heading to Selfridges one day to look at watches and she must have somehow caught wind of this because she rang me out of the blue. She mentioned she could get me a discount on a Rolex and told me to take a picture of one that I liked. It was when we met outside her office later on that she ran off for the present. My friend, photographer and soon to be film-maker Rufus had some inkling as to what was about to unfold as he'd already got the camera out and was waiting to capture my reaction. I opened the box to see a personalised Rolex – a matt-black submariner with green numerals, watch hands and my logo on the face. On the back she'd inscribed a heart with 'Love you long time, Lil x' in her own handwriting. I, for once, was at a loss for words.

I suppose that the Rolex was a symbol of changing times in more ways than one. Things were finally coming together. It's funny that she got me that watch as a thank-you: I know that I'll always have more to thank her for. I hope Lil looks back on those times we worked together as kindly as I do.

In September I made an appearance at the 2010 Bestival. I was back where it had all started with Lily a year earlier, this time to play a full gig under my own name. But it wasn't so much the performance that was memorable this time around. On the day I was playing, I was sitting backstage on a bench when I saw an extremely cute girl and her friend. I'm not sure who said, 'Hello,' first but we ended up talking and drinking for a while. Her name was Candy McCulloch and she had these cute cat ears on and somehow managed to make wellies look incredibly fashionable and hot. She was from Liverpool and had a cute Scouse accent along with a cute everything else. We spent the afternoon and early evening together before she and her friend Jordana came along to watch the gig. I ended up wearing the cat ears at one point and it became apparent quite quickly that there was something there.

There was something warm about her. She was polite, well-spoken, absolutely gorgeous and familiar with the business I was in because of her family history (her father was Echo and the Bunnymen frontman Ian McCulloch). We kissed and exchanged numbers before I had to leave. We next met after a session in which I recorded the song 'Trouble', which would appear on my second album. Chris Benns was again driving and we picked up Candy and her friend Jordana as they were visiting London for a night out. Candy was a great drinker and she wasn't on anything else. This suited me down to the ground as I was in the same place. But drink she could and I definitely found a drinking buddy in her. We had great times together and eventually we moved in together, first in Clerkenwell and then to a flat in Bermondsey Street – the first home of my own that wasn't council-owned.

And yet I couldn't entirely leave my past behind me. Just a few weeks after Bestival I got a reminder of the stabbing of more than 18 months earlier. In the aftermath of the attack I had said I hadn't wanted to press charges but the prosecution against the attacker rumbled on in the background – the CPS were taking on the case due to the severity of the crime. Out of the blue I heard the case was just about to come to court. The trial had already been postponed once and it was only when I got famous that the police developed more of an interest and moved the date to cause me maximum disruption, knowing they could capitalise on such a high-profile case with the press. I was in the middle of my debut headline tour, in Newcastle, when a copper called me. 'You're due in court next week.'

ARE YOU A REAL PROFESSOR?
9.

The trial of my attacker came to court and the police pressurised me to testify. Once I'd woken from surgery and the fact I'd been arrested had had time to sink in, my first thoughts were how hard it'd make travel if I was convicted of not just possession, but possession with intent – the close encounter with death had made me want to realise my dreams even more. It might sound stupid – I definitely feel stupid looking back – but I just thought, play the good citizen, play the sympathy card. I didn't think what I was caught with was enough to get put down for, but there were a few bits and bobs and pulling off personal use was a long shot. I really didn't have the foresight to think signing off on my statement, made up of ramblings to officers as I sat there on the curb bleeding and in shock, would later land me in court.

I was also in a very different position to the one I'd be

in by the time it got to court – something I had no way of predicting. If I'd been Mike Skinner or Example testifying it wouldn't have cost me a thing as far as reputation, but because of how I grew up I knew what was at stake. As if nearly dying wasn't enough suffering I made a stupid bloody decision which would later on add insult to injury, getting stabbed – the gift that kept on giving.

Giving evidence for the prosecution was something you just didn't do where I came from. It wouldn't matter why I did it – it wouldn't matter that I wasn't finger pointing because I'd been nicked and couldn't take the bird, nor that I hadn't started something and then ran to the police because I realised I'd bitten off more than I could chew. There was no history to the events that took place and I wasn't the aggressor. But none of this would matter. There would be a small percentage of people who wouldn't care about the details and would just see it in black and white. Others would be more understanding. A majority of the population would see testifying as the right thing to do, but it wasn't about what everyone else thought – it was about how I felt having to do something I was entirely uncomfortable with and then having to live with my decision, whether I felt I had a choice or not. My character would be smeared and I would be denounced if I went to court. But now it looked as if I had no choice. The police called me while I was in Newcastle on tour to tell me to turn up.

'I won't be turning up,' I said. 'I'm not coming.'

'You refuse,' the copper said. 'Okay, well, we know exactly where you are. Right now, you're in Newcastle, tomorrow you're in Brighton...' and he named all the cities on the tour itinerary. They were clearly keeping an eye on my career. He warned that the police would issue a summons, find me and arrest me if I didn't turn up. I lost my temper and told him that I was the one who had been stabbed and it shouldn't be me he was threatening. He made it very clear it wasn't a threat.

I got straight on the phone to Ged. We spoke to two barristers and found out where we stood. Nowhere good, it seemed: because I'd given a signed statement, legally I had to attend the trial. This may seem obvious to anyone familiar with the workings of the law but when I was involved in extra-curricular activities, I wasn't too bate about what I did. My dealings with the law were minimal, which for the most part was a positive. Until now. My statement had been entered into evidence and the attacker's defence had the right to cross-examine me. If I'd known that at the time I wouldn't have given a statement but now it was far too late.

I went through the options in my mind. If I was a no-show at court and arrested I would be forced to cancel gigs and I didn't think that missing my first headline performance in London would go down too well with the fans. My career would have been dealt a massive blow, Virgin themselves saying that failing to take the stand would be taken by the media as an act of cowardice rather than as holding up a code of not snitching. The negative publicity would affect my TV and radio support. The press loves to sensationalise and I could quite easily be portrayed as an advocate of knife crime. I'd be a scapegoat.

It had me tearing my hair out. There didn't seem to be a good way forward. Missing the shows wasn't an option. There was no insurance covering the cancellations so I'd have been in god knows how much more debt in an already strained financial situation, but that wasn't the point. I realised that I had a public profile and the responsibilities that go with it. And what a time to realise it. I went to court and reluctantly dotted the 'i's, crossed the fucking 't's and tried to put a full stop on the shittiest chapter of my life.

Before I had to give evidence I was talking to another witness who overheard me telling Ged how much I had wanted to walk out. He pulled me aside and told me the only reason he was giving evidence was because he saw a friend stabbed – fatally – in the same circumstances and he wanted to know how I could even consider not being there. It kind of hit home. The attacker was eventually sentenced to eight years, but would serve only two. I've spent a lot longer beating myself up over ever showing up, ridiculous when you think about the severity of what happened to me and how much pain it caused my family, but I reckon I've done enough of that now.

More positively, that month I got three nominations at the Mobos, for best newcomer, best song ('I Need You Tonight') and I won best hip-hop act. I thanked Ged and Simon for putting up with my shit during what was my first award acceptance speech, their wives too (love you, Ele, Lucy) and then went on to dedicate the award to Ryan Jarman's haircut and Kate Nash's second album. Don't ask. There were many other things I said that day to my nearest and dearest, soppiness which I won't repeat – but I meant it. It was good to be getting recognition, though I often felt that awards were often more about industry politics than the real meaning of the music. I prefer those chosen by the people although I'm not dismissive of awards in general. I later got a Brit nomination and I was definitely pleased to have that nod.

There were now two completely different sides to my life, best summed up by how I took to my first press shoot. I went temporarily blind. At first I thought I'd had some reaction to the make-up products but I realised it was down to the constant glare of the flash ring. I'd ended up with an equivalent of snow-blindness; my eyes were swollen and streaming for hours afterwards. That was my reaction to my small amount of fame.

I still walked my dog every morning and I'd say, 'Hello,' to people I bumped into regularly. Before, nobody had taken any notice of me but all of a sudden I'd get people saying, 'Ah, you're Professor Green. What are you doing round here?' Privately, I would be thinking, Hold on a minute, you've said, 'Hello,' to me every day for the past six months – do I look different?

There was a moment on a train too. I used to go to Stratford sometimes to get the overground to Liverpool Street and one day I sat down opposite some guy. The carriage was almost empty and he kept on staring at me. So I looked back at him, not screwfacing him but definitely not smiling. He kept bogging at me so I decided to err on the side of caution. Eventually, we got off the train and I was soon against the barriers getting my Oyster card out of my wallet. He came towards me and just as it was about to kick off – or so I thought – he said, 'Are you Professor Green?' All I could think was, Fucking hell.

From that point on I learned how to disarm situations, as much for myself as anyone. Some people want to say 'Hi' because they like my music, but don't know how to and are awkward; others have certain preconceptions about me or rappers in general and I prove that wrong just by being friendly. When it's not a response people expect, saying 'Hello' and smiling can be quite the tool.

It was the same approach that I took to the press. I'd been on the cover of *Hip-Hop Connection* when I was with The Beats and I'd had a good relationship with lots of people in magazines and websites who were passionate about the sort of music that I was making. Yet now I was in the mainstream media and I started to be asked the most banal and stupid questions, ones to which, despite my best intentions, I'd draw a complete blank. 'What would you be a professor of?' was a popular one to begin with. I was also regularly asked to go to the student unions at Oxford or Cambridge to give talks but I wasn't so keen on that idea. Give me a question and I'll answer it, but I'm not sure what I'd have to talk about in a speech. Maybe I could come to an arrangement with them – I'll write a paper and they can give me an honorary university post. That way, when people make a shit joke about me not really being a professor, I can say, 'Actually, I am.'

I would now also often be asked to rap on the spot. As I had freestyled and come up through battling, it began to feel like it was expected of me everywhere I turned. I accepted one challenge, from Ant and Dec, in a rap battle on their *Saturday Night Takeaway* for a laugh. There wasn't a ref but I reckon I won. Just. More often than not, though, I politely decline these days. When you're sat in a room with journalists on a conveyor belt, in and out all day, it's generally not the most inspiring of environments.

I began to notice that now I was getting well-known, photographers would try to take sly pictures of the scar on my neck. They'd never just ask though. It would always be, 'Oh, do you mind, you know, if we just like… er, could you look that way?' as if they were being really subtle and clever about it.

So I'd just take them straight on. 'Oh, you want to take a picture of where I got stabbed in the neck and nearly died?' I was never really angry about it. By that point I'd made my peace with what happened and I recognised that people found it morbidly fascinating – but a photographer's face when I confronted them like that was priceless. In that situation, at least, I can deal with awkward. It's fine when you're in control. Put me in a room watching a bad stand-up comedian, though, and I'll be so painfully uncomfortable I'll invert into my belly button.

I never had any media training to handle these situations as I got all I needed in one line from Lily Allen. During the video shoot for 'Just Be Good to Green' someone joked that I had to be more professional in interviews and Lily offered her advice! She said that if anyone ever asks me if I'm grateful for anything I should just say, 'Yeah, I really want to thank Peter Andre for looking after my children.' It's advice I've always followed. Maybe Lil should have some publishing on 'Monster'.

It was meeting people like Lily through music that was one of the best parts of finding success as far as I was concerned. New experiences were better than making more cash. Fair enough, money makes it easier to have those experiences, but it was the moments I shared with people that put the smile on my face. Money had always meant stress for me when I was young. I'd longed for material things when I watched rap videos as a kid, but as more money began to flow in, I realised that those things the young me had wanted were not that significant. Success felt good in itself. Musical recognition was something I'd risked everything for and worked my arse off to get and it felt good to be succeeding at something that was positive. That was decent. That was legal. That my nan could be proud of me for doing.

It was hard to keep track of all the people I was meeting. Sometimes I didn't realise until a moment had almost passed that it was something I should be filing away in my memory.

But that's the way it was. I couldn't live it and watch it at the same time, not those brief occasions when, say, I might be getting stuck into the whiskey at a do hosted by Jamie Oliver when Blur's Alex James offered, in an otherwise normal conversation, a blowjob. I laughed and said, 'Well, depends who it's from.' He kind of walked away awkwardly. I'm pretty sure he was joking. I hope he was joking. Or when I met Liam Gallagher by chance at a Levi's party where he immediately spun me around. I put my hand out to shake his and he put his fists up and started airboxing. 'Do you wanna slap me or shake my hand?' I said and he replied, 'Hey, Green, I couldn't give a fook about your rapping, right, but I like your tones. Take care of your voice.' Good advice and in some ways this sort of recognition from other musicians meant more to me than being nominated for and winning awards. But at the time such fleeting incidents and many others beside, were hard to appreciate in any meaningful way.

I didn't usually get flustered when I meet people but I remember tripping over my words the time I met Rosie Huntington-Whiteley after performing at the Elle Style Awards. I was just about to leave when a girl came up to me and asked if I'd mind going to say, 'Hello,' to her friend. I went over and I realised who it was and suddenly became conscious of every word barely coming out of my mouth. She asked me what performing was like and I said something along the lines of, 'It was cool' – smooth, I know – then asked her how it was to collect her award.

'Oh, I hated it,' she replied and made a downing-drinks gesture. 'My palms were sweating and everything.'

'Everything?' I replied. But it was probably a bit too early for jokes. A peck on the cheek and I was on my way to the lift.

My publicist, Phoebe Sinclair, had a mini-fit: 'She was playing with her hair! What the fuck just happened?' Apart from a slightly awkward conversation – not much. Though I was in control of the awkward so it was fine.

It was a really happy time. Something I suppose I'm more aware of looking back. The frequent anxiety and panic attacks made it harder to enjoy at the time, but I was aware of how different things could have been. Music had given me a voice and had altered the trajectory of my life. I was talking with Chyna the other day, discussing how at a certain point in your life you have to start living in the way you want your children to know you to be – and more importantly how you want them to live. The one thing we all shared growing up was that, essentially, we all had good hearts. We were all good kids in a sometimes bad area. Chyna and I went through a patch when we didn't talk but we eventually resolved our differences, not long before *Anuvahood* came out, the film he wrote (as Michael Vu) with another friend, Adam Deacon, whose flat we spent all those nights in. Sitting at the premiere was overwhelming, seeing a film on the big screen my friends had written and acted in – no small feat on their parts.

But as a crew we weren't as close as we once were. It was weird that people who'd been such a part of my journey were not there as things finally started to work. Danya and Karim, who I'd met through Ashley and who also played a big part both on screen and in producing the video for 'Jungle', were looking to serve, respectively, four years of a seven-year sentence and a heavy 14 years.

'Jungle' highlighted some of the negative aspects of where I grew up though it became the most important song for me on *Alive Till I'm Dead*. People seemed to have polarised attitudes to the song, but nobody could say that it wasn't true to life. I wanted the track to be a single but the record company preferred to stop at three with 'Monster'. I told them if I had to I'd put 'Jungle' out myself and the label were cool about it in the end. They just weren't interested because the nature of 'Jungle's' subject matter meant they were sure the song wouldn't get daytime radio play as a single. They gave me a few grand to do the video and pretty much left me to it.

My friend Ashley and I had known each other since we'd attended the same school for a while, although he'd been a few years above me. I happened to mention the video I was doing and he asked if he could be involved as it was his favourite track. I was still on tour so I put Ashley in touch with Henry Schofield, who had been responsible for most of my videos up to then and the legend that is James Hackett, the video commissioner for Virgin. I quickly turned in my performance shots between tour dates and had very little to do with the video before I saw the finished article. The film was very stark and uncompromising. Danya and Fifth both feature in the video and helped to put it together. Along with Ashley they brought out a load of the Clapton and Stamford Hill lot. Everything got a bit heated when the police decided to enter a flat in which they were filming in. Luckily, the video was completed without any arrests.

And then the song that was definitely going to be marked not for radio was added to Radio 1's playlist over Christmas. Very festive. In some ways I was as surprised as the record company in that I could see it wasn't an obvious daytime song but it ended up A-listed all over the holidays and now the record company looked at the clip and were suddenly in a panic. Having told me I could do what I wanted with a video they hadn't been interested in before they only realised now that it was totally unsuitable. Why haven't we go something we can get on TV? they wanted to know. It was a bit late for all that. In the end, despite the lack of a showable video, 'Jungle' got to UK No 31 after its release in January. It was the last single from the album, which had by then itself already sold over 270,000 copies.

'Jungle' was also a bit of a breakthrough for me with the *NME* as I've had an up-and-down relationship with the magazine over the years. But in February, the single got an *NME* award for best dancefloor filler. My nan holds on to all my trophies and sales discs and the one from the *NME* went straight into her place as well. Except that it didn't go in the front room – the *NME*'s trophy is a cast of a hand giving a middle-finger salute so that stays in her bedroom when she has visitors.

I was able to maintain the vibe of 'Jungle' when I was asked to do a song for an ad campaign. It was for Doritos and they'd thought of me as they were doing a range aimed at late night snacking. They actively wanted me to come up with a track that had something of the night about it. It was to accompany an interactive video shot on a new kind of 360-degree camera. Give us something 'dark', they asked. As I'd shown with 'Jungle', I could always do dark and 'Coming To Get Me' took its cue from the mood and approach of that earlier track.

Recording the song formed a kind of bridge into the second album, *At Your Inconvenience*. It had come around quickly; activity around the first album continued well into 2011 – promotion, interviews, recording, gigging – and it was happening without me needing to try for it. I was moving into a phase where I was beginning to step into the world of 'celebrity'. Still a word I'm uncomfortable with. Along with the gathering chart success, gigs and music shows, I began being asked to do TV shows, at first music-based programmes such as *Never Mind the Buzzcocks*, which I did a few times. My favourite experience on *Buzzcocks* was my first, that January, when Frankie Boyle was hosting for a second time. Luckily, Frankie likes me, because he's one of the sharpest, most merciless comedians out there and I wouldn't like to be the subject matter of his humour. I also have to say his knowledge of hip-hop is pretty fucking impressive. Michelle from Destiny's Child was on the panel. She was very, very religious and also very American. She just didn't get the super-British, utterly profane shitstorm going on around her in the slightest and I'm not quite sure how she tolerated it.

A lawyer from the BBC – perhaps brought in specifically to monitor Frankie Boyle because he wasn't there for other episodes – stood just off-camera going, 'Yep, we can use that,' and 'Nope, we'll have to reshoot.' Frankie wasn't interested in the autocue at all. His ad-libbed introduction ran, 'It's the second time I've hosted *Never Mind The Buzzcocks* and, I must say, I do feel a bit like a murderer who's returned to the scene of the crime… to have a wank.' I moved on from music shows to do programmes such as *BBC Breakfast* and even *Loose Women* – quite a departure from the stark nature of the 'Jungle' video.

I recorded the album in a six-month block without a break in the schedule alongside everything else. Holed up in the studio, I didn't bother keeping my hair short as I usually did. I'd always cut it myself or gone to a Turkish barber's and got a shave and a really tight cut. Now I looked like a fucking scruff-bag but I wasn't going anywhere so it didn't really matter until a shoot came up for *Esquire* magazine. I was to model ten different looks that included clothes I would never otherwise wear – at one point I even sported a pair of very visible orange socks. It was a different experience for me as I wasn't usually experimental in what I wore (white t-shirt, jeans and Varsity jacket were pretty much me). But it was the hair that really took me outside my fashion comfort zone.

The hair stylist (Oliver Wood, who did hair for his close friend Robbie Williams) explained that the first look was to be 1950s and asked if I minded if he did something with my hair before he cut it off? I was doubtful. He could try but I was pretty sure I wouldn't like it. Permission granted, he gave me a quiff. 'Bruv, I don't know about this,' I said. 'This is a bit much.' He knew where I was from and he'd heard the music as much as anyone else. He should have known that a quiff didn't really fit. But as the women on the shoot passed by, from fashion editor Catherine Hayward to Phoebe my publicist, each said with genuine surprise, 'Wow – that really suits you.' I decided it could stay for the day. The new look got its first major public outing in the video for 'At Your Inconvenience' and became quite a talking point – thankfully, more positive than negative – and I started to gather a strong female following.

Writing the album was an intensive process and when it was at its height my relationship with Candy suffered – or at least I told myself our difficulties were down to the impossibility of keeping a relationship going while creating a record. We split up while remaining friends, although I was left feeling unsure whether or not we'd made the right move in parting. I put my difficult emotions into some highly charged tracks on the record and that made them hard to make, no more so than 'Read All About It'.

'Read All About It' began with a chorus written by Ian James and producers TMS that Sam Evitt had sent to me, telling me to listen to it with an open mind. I loved the lyrics but the track had quite an upbeat, R&B-ish kind of vibe. It was all very happy – I wanna sing, I wanna shout – and this was at a particularly hard time for me.

My dad's widow, Jackie, had made a reappearance in my life. I had managed to keep my distance from her, being civil when we needed to be in contact, but I'd wanted to put the distressing aspects of my dad's life behind me and her along with them. As far as I was concerned she wasn't family and she wasn't anything to do with me. Then I heard that she had sold a story to one of the tabloids claiming that I had cashed in on his death to further my career. She said that I should have known that she didn't want 'her husband's' death discussed and accused me of profiting from it.

I was sickened: she'd twisted my success in music – which was positive and an achievement that I would have loved more than anything to share with my dad – into something shameful and grubby. Maybe she never knew I'd been hurting so much by not having my father around and maybe she didn't realise what hurt the article caused me. But even if she had been right and I had wanted to commercialise his death in some way, why would I wait until I already had a successful album and tour? It didn't make sense. I didn't need the publicity.

By now I'd got to the point where I could talk about my dad's death when it mattered – in relation to how people suffer from depression, for example – but it still pained me every time I was reminded of what happened to him. So to be accused of cynically exploiting his death was devastating. It confirmed to me everything I'd thought about Jackie and reminded me of why I hadn't wanted anything to do with her.

The emotion poured out in 'Read All About It' – you can hear the sadness, anger and defiance. I almost feel as though I should thank Jackie – she inspired my most successful song to date! I won't though.

I've never been keen on explaining my words or what a song means to me, but 'Read All About It' is the exception. I still feel strongly about what happened with Jackie. Usually I think an artist's best songs are their most personal and the ones most open to interpretation – a good example being a favourite of mine, 'The Drugs Don't Work' by the Verve. It was originally about Richard Ashcroft's terminally ill father, the medication no longer working and his suffering while waiting for the inevitable end. But you can also interpret it as being a song about addiction. Yet you don't even need an explanation – the song transcends language: it could be just be a melody and I think you'd still get a sense of the melancholy and the heartache it expresses. At its best it sets a scene and creates a mood and when it works it doesn't need explaining.

Mostly, I think people should be allowed to make up their own minds and interpret songs how they want. In my own work, 'Astronaut' mixes together two stories of people I've known struggle with heroin. And I hadn't had the runaround in a relationship that was the subject of 'I Need You Tonight'. You don't need to know exactly what inspired most of my songs to find them as true as 'Read All About It', even if that track did have a very specific story. But its direct emotional content required a more sombre feel when it came to recording. Sadly, by this point Harry-Lloyd Jones, Sam Evitt and Jack had left Virgin. The label's future was then uncertain and they were among many people who departed. I was handed to Glyn Aikens, who did my A&R and, along with producers TMS,

Jules Buckley and the Heritage Orchestra and later Ishi, who did additional production, we worked to create a darker vibe that was more in keeping with what I wanted to express. When Emeli agreed to sing the chorus everything was in place for one of my most heartfelt tracks.

Royce da 5'9" was among the other collaborators on the album, on 'Nightmares'. We recorded our parts separately on our different sides of the Atlantic – and we would do it the same way when I did Flexplicit's 'My Games' with him the following year – he would later pay me a huge compliment on Twitter out of the blue. He's someone I (along with pretty much every other rapper) respect greatly for his penmanship. Getting to do a couple of songs with him was a standout of all the collaborations I've done. I've been lucky enough to work with Wretch 32, Ghetts, Giggs, Tinie, Big Narstie, Plan B, Example, Mike Skinner... it's a long list. Alongside the Royce da 5'9" tracks, I'd say that 'Game Over', the Tinchy Stryder record I did in 2010, was also up there. I got on that through Benny Scarrs, who did the A&R for the record and who I knew from Jump Off days. He called when I was on the Eurostar on the way to do some promo and asked me if I was up for jumping on the song along with the likes of Example, Giggs and Tinie Tempah. The only catch was that I had to deliver my verse in 24 hours. I had the words within ten minutes but there was still the issue of having to record it while he was in Jersey for a gig the next day. We managed to fly Alex out with a portable studio and get it done in the hotel room.

In collaborating I take inspiration when I look back to that golden era of early 90s hip-hop when everyone worked together. Everyone was on each other's tracks, mixing in the same studios, shit just happened – often spontaneously. Rappers are competitive, so you're always going to want to better the next man. No matter how friendly you are with them, if you get on a song with someone you get on it to fucking win.

Other songs on the album included 'Spinning Out', a Pixies-sampling track that had its origins in a Biz Session for *The Sun*. It was after midnight on the day of the session when I was sent into a panic as I re-read an email and realised I also had to perform a cover. A lot of coffee and a very late night followed and I had managed to write the remix – leaving time only to rehearse the song with the band in soundcheck. I drew from exactly what was going on for me at the time. A lot was changing and that's reflected in the lyrics – I sneaked a bit of wordplay in there too, 'Women coming in pairs [pears] and I'm enjoying the fruits of my success.' I later recorded it with Fink and his band. The Pixies were kind enough to clear the sample with the condition we changed the title of the song from 'Where is My Mind?' and it became a key song on the album. Rufus made a video using footage we'd acquired over the years, a lot of it previously unseen.

My approach to recording in the studio remained fluid and loose. I would leap between ideas and tracks in a way that Alex found difficult to deal with. He wasn't alone – I first started work on 'Read All About It' with an MP3 of the track from the record company and strict instructions not to get sidetracked. But when I got to the studio TMS played me a clip of what would become 'Trouble' among the other material. I'd loved jungle ever since I was a kid and ended up using up our time to write and record that one instead. I was happy because it sounded sick and it was the first song I'd finished for the album. Everyone else was like, 'Can you just fucking finish "Read All About It", please?' There's no pleasing some people.

We made time for great parties between sessions. One sticks in the memory because I lost my newly bought and highly prized Margiela jacket or, at least, thought I did. I'd come home after a fairly unsuccessful date. The chick in question turned up pissed where we started near my flat in Bermondsey Street. She got increasingly drunk and I could see things were going badly. I suggested we go on as my friend Danny Chan was at a pub in Covent Garden. I sneaked off to the toilet and called him to ask if he'd crash the date.

He was late but we eventually headed to visit the Hoxton Pony where we bumped into people the girl worked with, as well as Lewis and Jon Calabrese, who owned the Pony. I thought I'd lost her, but as we were getting into a cab she showed up again. I made out that I had just been coming back to get her. We all went to the Groucho for a bite to eat – I thought it might help sober her up – but there was no such luck, she just started making a mess with her food. Luck did however strike when we got into a venue called The Box and again bumped into the people she worked with – I left her with them as I said we were off to get a table and she didn't show up again.

As we left a couple of hours later, the paps started snapping and caught the attention of a nearby transvestite, who ran up and put his arm around me. By this time I was in no mood for messing around. 'Get the fuck off me!' I said.

He decided to tease me. 'What are you doing in the middle of gay-town then Prof – Poof Green!' As I cocked back my arm in cartoon fashion, Lewis hooked my arm and stuffed me into a black cab.

We got back to my flat to find a full-blown party. I had no idea what was going on. 'How the fuck did you lot get back here before me? And how did you get into my flat!' A good few hours passed in a blur and as people started leaving I went to my room to find two people asleep in the bed. Right then, spare bed it is, I thought, but that was gone too. Lewis and a mate of his were top and tailing with Alfie the dog in the middle.

I bedded down in the carnage of the living room but it seemed only seconds later that I was being roasted by the heat of the morning sun. I got up for a piss and welcomed the cooler atmosphere at the back of the flat. It was too much to resist. I took a pair of tracksuit bottoms from the washing basket, climbed into the bath using the joggers as a pillow and fell asleep. I woke around 1 pm, more or less refreshed, with the urge to go get a roast, and as we were about to head out the door, thought, Hold on a second, where's my Margiela blazer? I'd only just bought it the day before.

Half an hour later, with the help of my old pal Danny Chan, I'd turned the house upside down and was just reaching the point of peak anger and despair when a voice in my head suggested I look in the freezer. And, yes, the fucking jacket was in there. I'd got chewing gum on it and, fucked as I was the night before, I'd thought to put it in to try and limit the damage. Didn't work, by the way. I had to take it to the dry cleaners but at least I still had it. That's what the nights were often like at that point: ditched my date, nearly had a fight with a tranny, slept in the bath, found my clothes in the freezer. Normal.

10.

EAST TO SOUTH WEST

The grieving process is strange. It never really stops. My dad had been dead for three years when we played as part of the Summer Sessions season in the grounds of Somerset House in London in 2011. We played 'Goodnight' for the first time, the track that had started off being about my struggles after my nanny Edie died and that I only finished after my dad's death. It would have been Carl playing keys that night and as soon as he started to play the intro I felt a flood of emotion I'd long kept at bay. That night was the only time I played the song live.

Somerset House is an imposing, former government building in the classical style that dates back to the 18th century. The gigs take place in its grand courtyard and we chose the venue over other London festivals because we wanted to do something different and to make a statement. The weather was threatening but the rain held off all day for that gig. We hit the stage knowing we had another sold-out show under our belt – I bounced out and, when I first talked to the crowd, I mentioned the history of the building. Years before they would have seen Nelson with his horse and carriage, now here was a toe-rag in a Puma tracksuit – not quite sure what my point was but the crowd went along with it. We brought along the orchestra for the encore and saved 'Goodnight' till last, ending the show with the song that finishes my first album.

The build-up to the release of the next album was charted in a six-part Channel 4 series, *Professor Green Unseen*, that followed Team Green as preparations continued and mischief was made. This was my second TV series, the first being *PGTV* on YouTube – as with the music side of things, I was doing it myself long before a big company got involved. Even earlier, I used to make clips myself, just silly little things, sometimes even using the built-in camera on the laptop. I had always wanted to do more. When I joined The Beats we made clips for the YouTube channel they'd devised called Beat Stevie. Smart name, even smarter characters. There was one clip of everyone at the label hanging out at Reading Festival where Mike was performing – Example had an accident with some pills when, having not done them before, took three in a row waiting for something to happen. The messy results were captured on film and still exist somewhere in the dark depths of the internets where they can be seen by all.

When it came to *PGTV* I approached Rufus, who had been a photographer, and asked him if he was any good with a video camera. He said he wasn't but was up for giving it a go. We began documenting everything and quickly gathered a strong following once we started uploading the debauchery to You Tube. The Channel 4 series wasn't half as fun as working solely with Rufus, simply because he got much more out of me as a result of being such a good mate, but it was strange to have our own TV show, especially with the freedom Channel 4 allowed us. None of us acted up for the camera – that was the charm of what we did, it was natural and it was easy to be so because it was made among friends. We had an explicit version that went out at midnight on a Monday as well as a Sunday morning version (though they must have had trouble finding enough footage for the pre-watershed show at times).

Unfortunately, doing the Channel 4 show meant that we subsequently let *PGTV* slide. We were focused on the TV show, though when the first series finished, the label hadn't wanted to follow-up with a second series as there wasn't a new album to promote. All of a sudden there was no TV show and not much was going up online. I didn't push on with it as I had so much else to do and now thinking about it I was an idiot for letting it slide. Everything I've achieved has come through doing stuff for myself or with my friends for ourselves. If I leave things to the label then things inevitably don't happen as quickly and being led by the label has sometimes been an excuse I've made for my own laziness.

Professor Green Unseen was itself a lot of work and had its serious moments, the hardest for me coming when they caught a discussion I had with MistaJam, Peter, who I know very well. I was usually able to disconnect myself from my emotions when I spoke about my dad in public, but because it was with Peter, I guess my guard was down and we had a very personal discussion. This was shot at the beginning of the

'Read All About It' promo and so everything was still pretty raw – you could hear in my voice it was getting to me. I totally forgot where I was as we were speaking.

I came out of the room feeling drained to find the producer suddenly in my face, grinning cheerfully. 'That was great!' he said. 'That was just what we needed.' And he made a thumbs-up gesture. I had to take a moment to control myself and just about managed a neutral response. From that moment on it became awkward and not long afterwards he was taken off the job. We eventually ended up with a really good crew on the programme, although I did have a further problem with someone else, a senior manager at the production company, when they thought I was going to be late for a shoot.

The filming had been going smoothly and I hadn't missed a day, but then I was in the car on the way to a shoot in Herne Bay on the coast with Chris Benns when we played a tiny, little, small joke on Rufus. I was just leaving my place in Bermondsey Street, a one-way street. I was behind a rubbish truck and there was traffic behind us – we couldn't move anywhere. The rubbish was being put in the back so it wasn't going to take long to clear but Rufus had the bad luck to phone just as we were sat there waiting. The devil in me took over: 'I don't know what to do,' I said. 'There's been an accident in front of us and we can't move anywhere. We're stuck.'

Rufus had a proper hissy fit. He was getting shit from this senior bloke at the production company as he was involved in the filming as well as being a character in his own right as my friend and colleague. So he was under double pressure, being filmed as he was filming. This muppet said to Rufus, 'I will end Stephen's relationship with Channel 4 if he does not get here.' That did not go down well with me when it was later relayed.

I filed it away in my mind, making a note to take it up with the bloke when I got the chance.

Rufus had his knickers in a twist until at last Chris phoned again with me in the car to confess all as we drove. Rufus didn't laugh but we did get to Herne Bay on time. This was quite a typical bit of mischief for me and Chris as a pair and we were laughing our arses off when we saw Rufus – but by this time he'd dealt with so much shit he didn't manage so much as a smile.

The big hurry? We had to shoot a scene on a boat owned by Trevor, who does my security. The idea was that Team Green would be sailing out on Trevor's boat to enjoy a relaxing afternoon's fishing in the bay – hard-working entertainers kicking back. Except that the sea was rough that day and everyone was sick as a dog. Anyone who wasn't throwing up over the side of the boat was puking in it. My crew, the TV crew, everyone was having a right mare. I felt just as bad but had no intention of admitting it to anyone and sat there pretending I was absolutely fine.

We eventually made it back to dry land and went to Trevor's local pub to cook our catch. The idea was to whip up a breaded seafood dish to conclude our perfect day off. First the fish had to be gutted, something I'd never done before. I took a tight hold of the fish and began to draw the knife down, but it must have needed to go to the toilet before it was caught, as a gloopy, revolting mass of dead fish shit spilled out of it. A disgusting experience – but at least I can now say I've gutted a fish.

One of my driving lessons was filmed in another segment for the show. I was accompanied by Charlotte De Carle, a model who I'd been friends with for a while who I met through Chris.

It would be this driving lesson (however staged) that would make Mini go back on their offer of giving me a car when I later passed my test due to some 'issues' they had with my driving. Ended up being a touch as not long after I bought a Mercedes I started to work with them. Fuck you, BMW!

I would next see the melon who was going to 'end my relationship with Channel 4' at the end of the red carpet at that year's Mobos. He was all smiles then and asked me how I was. I slowed down just enough to whisper in his ear that we needed to have a fucking word and walked on. But I never saw him again. Next thing I heard, he had been fired. Poor guy. It wasn't anything to do with what had happened with me and I never got to find out why he felt the need to be so aggressive. How could he end my relationship with Channel 4 anyway? I'd had a great relationship with them and it continues to this day. Shame his didn't.

I played quite a few gigs over the summer. On one Saturday in July I played the Oxegen festival in Ireland and was on the boat to T in the Park for a show the next day when I had a bite of scrambled egg that included a piece of tough eggshell. I snapped a tooth and booked in with my dentist who assured me I could have an implant and be fine after 24 hours. Bollocks. My gum swelled up until it split. I was put on metronidazole and I was very open with my dentist about my plans for an Ibiza trip later that week. He warned me that this was the one antibiotic I couldn't drink alcohol while I was taking, but said it was fine as I'd be off it in time.

We played Benicassim and then came the two-week holiday in Ibiza I'd booked for everyone. I ended up on the antibiotics for the whole fucking fortnight! I spent the whole time watching people party without touching a drop, let alone any of the island's other offerings. It felt like being on a big family holiday, the kind I'd never had as a kid. There were about ten or 12 of us at the villa along a dusty track in the middle of nowhere. We'd take it in turns to cook (except IQ, who I'm not sure knew how to), sitting around the big wooden table on the terrace from morning till night, telling stories. When we went out, it was as a group. I got to watch everyone else get off their nuts while I sat content with the codeine I'd been prescribed for the tooth pain. Being forced to stay clean, I came out of the break feeling better than I did at the start. I'd never left Ibiza feeling quite so revitalised.

Back home I got to thank INXS in person for being so good about clearing the sample of 'I Need You Tonight'. Keyboardist Andy Farriss and I had emailed back and forth, and a personal rapport had developed between us, so when I heard they were just round the corner from my house, rehearsing for a show on Clapham Common, I popped in with the dog to say, 'Hello'. It was a brief visit as I didn't want to interrupt, but it was great to shake their hands and thank them for being kind enough to let me sample one of their classics, let alone to agree on such a fair deal. They'd played a part in my first hit and to meet them was one of those moments.

I was still missing Candy and, despite all our problems, I regretted having stopped seeing her while I was working on the album. But in truth it had probably only been an excuse to say that recording didn't leave space for the relationship. I just wasn't coping well – both with the changes in my life as well as with issues from my past I hadn't dealt with. My anxieties and stresses related as much to my childhood as to everything happening around me. I was self-medicating with an ever-increasing intake of Valium. We gave it another go, but it wasn't to be. Candy is one of the kindest and most caring women I've come across but I was probably just a little bit too numb to everything at the time. I wasn't at the point where I could deal with someone who knew how to love me. I related love and passion to fighting, having arguments and headaches as my prior relationships had been full of those. Felix moved into the place we had shared in east London's Repton Park. He had been living with his aunt and had been looking for somewhere of his own so it made perfect sense.

It was around the same time Lewis also split up with his missus and moved in shortly before the tenancy was due to expire. The Repton Park development was a conversion of the former Claybury psychiatric hospital, set in beautiful grounds which Lewis nevertheless found to be creepy at night: he never liked to be in the old asylum on his own. I have to admit, I wasn't too fond of being in it on my own either. There was a time when this weird noise could be heard and Alfie the dog would just sit in the corner of the living room looking at a blank wall. Turned out it was an owl, but still. There were many parties and a few indiscretions, as befitted a house of single men. As a trio we became a real tight unit, family more than the friends we'd been since childhood. We weren't always well-behaved, but we looked after each other.

When we had to move on we decided to keep our household together. My soon-to-be ex-landlord wanted to take lots of money off me for various claims he made about the house but he didn't realise I had taken screenshots of all our discussions via text. I sent him the images and got the deposit back the next day – cheers, landlord Aftab.

After much looking around London we moved more centrally and rented a house near World's End on Lots Road,

Chelsea. You'd have to try quite hard to find somewhere in that area that was next to council flats but we somehow managed to. We only had a small kitchen so we didn't do that much cooking at home and the chaos we'd first caused in Repton Park soon began to mature in the pubs and bars of south west London.

At Your Inconvenience came out in the last part of 2011. 'Read All About It' was the lead single, released in October just ahead of the album. Early excitement around the track had created a huge buzz. It felt like a comeback single even though it hadn't been that long since we'd last released something. There was a sense of anticipation from fans but then came a weird moment, a week before release, when it felt like it might have plateaued, but fortunately it was a false alarm as the single hit the No 1 spot, the first of my songs ever to do so. A moment we captured for *Professor Green Unseen*, the last day's filming we'd do for it, in fact, just as we were rehearsing to go on tour. A perfect end if there ever was one.

Soon after I found myself slated to perform 'Read All About It' on both the most commercial and then the most credible music show on telly in the same week, almost by accident. I had wanted to film live sessions of tracks from the album and my TV pluggers at the time, Vic and Rob, sent 'Astronaut' to *Later*, who loved it. But meanwhile, over at *X Factor*, celebrity producer Liz Holmwood was relentlessly playing 'Read All About It' at her production meetings week after week until finally everyone agreed I should go on. So that became the chosen track.

Going on *X Factor* was one of the few things that have made me nervous. I knew the roll call of names that have filled the guest slot and I didn't feel I was in the same league as some of the other big performers. On the morning of the show I was up at 7 am and already at my nan's, drinking tea and talking about absolutely nothing while trying to distract myself from the nervous energy I could feel building. Nan came with me. The studio, which appears huge on screen, is actually tiny. At the time Dermot O'Leary was the host and he was a proper sweetheart. He made the time to come and say, 'Hello,' to my nan before I went on stage. To say she swooned would be an understatement.

I couldn't help thinking about all the millions of people watching as I waited anxiously to walk out. That appearance joined a lot of dots in people's minds and pushed the single to my first UK No 1. For two weeks after *X Factor*, 'Read All About It' wouldn't budge from the top of iTunes. That was too overwhelming to digest. I can't begin to describe what it felt like, though the joy was somewhat bittersweet given what I'd endured to be able to write that song. We later did a version for Italy with an artist called Dolcenera singing the hook in Italian. It went platinum and led to me performing at the San Remo music festival, doing a version of a well-known Italian song with Dolcenera, produced by Cores, called '*Vita Spericolata*', or 'Reckless'.

I had a day full of promo on the Monday after *X Factor* and on Tuesday I went straight into rehearsals in the *Later* studio. To my left in the studio were Coldplay and in a quiet moment Chris Martin came across and said, 'Man, we were saying "Swear down" on the tour bus for a whole summer.' That was a head-fuck. Chris Martin from Coldplay quoting from 'I Need You Tonight'? What? It was surreal. As with the casual nod from Liam Gallagher, this kind of acceptance from other artists meant a great deal to me. On *Later* we ended up playing 'Astronaut' alongside 'Read All About It', with Emeli again contributing her part.

As we got ready to promote the album on the road, it was without Chris Benns. He had been my tour manager and right-hand man since we'd worked together on my independent videos, but his long-term partner was due to have a baby at the start of the tour. He started off doing the tour but soon heard that his newborn wasn't doing too well – although the child went on to be fine – and he had to be present at home a lot more than he might otherwise have been. Within two days he came to me to say that his partner needed him for a while. I knew that he wasn't going to be able to stay for the rest of the dates and I told him that, to be honest, I wasn't surprised that it hadn't turned out to be a good idea. I completely understood that he needed to be with his young family.

As Chris left for daddy duties, Felix fell into the roll of tour manager and hype man after a party we did on the London Eye. Red Bull had organised an event called Revolution Sound, with each pod on the big wheel containing a sound system, a musician, a well-stocked bar and enough people to make a party. Wretch 32 had a pod, Miss Dynamite had one too and so did Skream and Benga.

The London Eye normally takes 30 minutes to do a complete rotation but it had been slowed to an hour for the party. Add to that some inconsiderate bastard from another pod getting off for a piss and my set finished before we made it round. IQ was DJing and, rather than let the vibe die down, Felix jumped on the mic and proceeded to completely turn that pod over. There were 20 or 30 people in there, dancing and drinking and Felix stood on the seat in the middle banging on the roof until something went wonky and cracked. Not bad going – breaking the London Eye by the sheer force of party. As fun as it was I doubt we'll be invited back any time soon (not least of all because I went on to work with Red Bull's competition, Relentless, for years). As we came to a stop and de-podded, Trevor quickly hustled me out to the car. Once Felix worked out where we'd gone, he joined us and I asked him to come and be hype man on the tour, warming up every night with DJ IQ.

Felix had a natural knack for looking out for others and was a straight shooter. As he did with everything, he quickly excelled at the job and has since looked after 5SOS during a stadium tour of the UK as well as various other acts that are far more successful than I am. I'm not the easiest person to look after when I get into my, erm, groove, but he's never not got us to where we need to be on time. Felix has seen me in some fucking states, although there was later one notorious evening when the tables were turned and I had to pull over quick sharp to save the lovely black-and-red leather interior of my Mercedes SLS from his vomit. Or at least I thought I had saved it, until I'd got him home and gave it a closer inspection. But this is definitely not the sort of behaviour he's renowned for and I reckon he more than deserves the occasional blowout for all the time he spends looking out for others. He was The Wolf of the gang, but he looked much sharper than Harvey Keitel in a tux.

We were now a slightly more sophisticated operation on the road and had a tour bus to take us around. The first of what would be many dates began with a crossing of the Irish Sea and the journey came after we'd been smoking heavily. IQ certainly looked really fucking ropy as we slowly assembled in the bus the morning after. He hadn't been in the slightest bit helped by a really choppy voyage and we arrived in Dublin with him looking very green. Then someone said there were sniffer dogs outside the coach. It was normal tour procedure for us all to take the piss out of each other mercilessly and play practical jokes, so nobody took the warning seriously until the dogs were almost all the way up the steps into the bus. Everyone was roused out of their stupor and we all had to file out and stand on the tarmac awkwardly. The stench was overpowering. And yet they didn't find anything. How we got away with it I'll never know. The only thing I can think of is that the odour was so strong that the dog just couldn't pinpoint it. A dog's nose is 20,000 times more powerful than a human's – even your gran would have been able to sniff out the weed (let alone my nan who, as you know, had become pretty wise to it). Maybe they were looking for something else but, thankfully, there was nothing except weed.

Touring was, as always, unpredictable, not least in the way that gig dynamics always changed, seemingly without reason. Sometimes the band all felt the same thing. The same energy from the crowd. But being on stage was also a very personal experience. There were times when I got back to the dressing room almost in despair because I felt I'd had the worst gig ever, but the band were fucking buzzing. Or I'd have had a great show and my drummer would be unhappy with something. Just sometimes we weren't in the right place to enjoy it. At times I worried too much and would find myself trying to make everything perfect. I would get concerned when even small things weren't right on stage or when I had feared I had a lurking sore throat, worrying I'd lose my voice.

I did try and be healthy, as I do at the start of most tours. I had Trevor put us under a proper boot camp and we worked out in the mornings, drinking green juices and being all pipe-and-slippers in the evenings, but as ever, it didn't last. Maybe that was no bad thing. When I was a bit less healthy, enjoying myself more with the Jack flowing (I could have given Slash from Guns n' Roses a run for his money – quite often half the bottle was gone before I was even on stage), the audience felt it and enjoyed the show more. Or maybe it was just me?

I had a bedroom at the front of the tour bus and after a Brighton show two girls came back on board. Things were starting to get interesting but then one of them out of nowhere said that she didn't feel very well. She must have misjudged her booze consumption and I could see what was about to happen. Her face turned from happy to woozy and I shouted for some help to get her off the bus. Two of us managed to help her outside and we sat on a bench while she puked. She was apologising and puking, 'I'm so sorry,' she repeated between heaves, 'I'm so sorry,' and all I could do was nurse her round, hold her hair back and tell her to relax. Once she'd come round I saw her and her friend into a cab and that was that.

At another venue I was with a girl when I managed to scare a member of the team. We were in the dressing room with, not to put too fine a point on it, my arse facing the door. The woman who did the merchandise came in to ask me something, then kind of stood there in shock when she realised what was happening. All I could think of, before I got carried away, was to say, 'Do you mind closing the door on the way out please?' And she left rather sheepishly.

Later, I was talking to the band and they said she'd come to see them half laughing, because it was so funny, but also crying, because she thought she'd committed some terrible sin and she was going to lose her job. 'Was he on his way in or out?' the band asked.

'What?'

'Clenched or unclenched?'

'Clenched.'

What could I do to let her know it was all right without causing more embarrassment? The next day I saw her, and as I was leaving the room, walked out with a fair portion of my derrière exposed. I think that worked, as she just started laughing. 'Don't worry, it's fine,' I said, hoping a moony didn't count as sexual harassment.

In November, Emeli performed at the Royal Albert Hall and filmed the gig. I was invited along to perform with her. It was weirdly intimidating; there with rows of people sitting down quietly to enjoy the show. I'd performed at the Albert Hall before when it was a lot less organised. Now you could definitely feel the pressure what with all the cameras around. I was to feature on her version of 'Read All About It' and I went on wondering if the crowd had even heard the original. But as soon as I appeared the dynamic changed and everyone got out of their seats. Another on the list of big performances with Emeli.

She went on to support Coldplay in Europe on the *Mylo Xyloto* tour and I was invited to join her for a few dates towards the end of the year. Chris Martin was again really friendly – not only did he drop my name into a song but I also had the chance to talk some more with him. He was very inquisitive and he even started asking me about my dad, which was bizarre given that we barely knew each other. I found myself wondering how we got to that point so quickly. But he was quite funny about it too. 'Man, don't you ever commit suicide. If you ever give it a thought just give me a shout and we'll go for a pizza.' Cheers, Martin, I will, though you never did give me your phone number.

Touring with Coldplay was something else. They'd done so well so quickly – I still travelled by tour bus but within a couple of years of getting together they'd quickly graduated to flying everywhere. They'd finish shows and while the audience were still filing out of the stadium the band would be in the van, on the way to the airport and waiting for them would be their plane. No eight-seater propeller plane for Coldplay, though. The one on which we were lucky enough to fly with them back to London could probably have seated 80 people! I sat behind Chris on board and we chatted about our current albums. 'So, what's the next single gonna be?' he asked. 'It's got to be "DPMO". Don't piss me off!'

In turn, I loved their track 'Up in Flames'. There was something Mike Skinnerish about it. 'That's gotta be yours,' I said. I didn't pick 'DPMO'. And they didn't pick 'Up In Flames' either. A mistake on both our parts...

At home I got back on the road in my own capacity to take my driving test. But on the evening of the very day I passed, I got stopped and was recognised by the police, though thankfully for my music rather than any previous encounters. I had been driving down the Mile End Road with Felix in my grey VW Polo – the car that made an appearance in the driving lesson they shot for *Professor Green Unseen*. One of the two coppers who stopped us, a young one, was trying to give me shit because I didn't have my licence on me and because I wasn't yet on the system, but his older colleague was more understanding of our story and shut up his junior muppet... but not without ripping the piss out of me for being a chart-topping musician and yet cruising around in an old Polo. Cunts. I wish they'd pulled me over in my SLS.

But then people often had wildly inaccurate ideas about how much money a rapper in the charts had. It was easy for people to make assumptions when I turned up to expensive restaurants or clubs in a £190k car, wearing a £20k watch and a £3k jacket. Especially when those people didn't realise the car was part of an endorsement, the watch took me two albums to afford, the jacket was gifted and the venue would comp everything once I got inside as a thank-you for the media attention they would receive from the pictures by the snap-happy paps. I guess what I'm working up to talking about here is working-class guilt – I'd come from fuck-all and, in what seemed to outsiders to be a short space of time, I had made a success of myself (the reality was eight years' graft and earning nothing for it). People assumed I had way more than I did and I felt like I had to explain every single penny I'd made, spent or didn't have – not a million miles away from what I'm doing right now!

A lot of people depended on me, both professionally and otherwise. I was under pressure not just to write hit songs – which was stressful enough – but to deal with everything that came with my success, quite often including everyone else's problems. I was at the top of a very fragile pyramid. It sometimes felt as if everyone thought they were my only friend and that I didn't have to consider anyone else. Expectations ran way too high. People would focus only on the benefits of the job. I used to, when I was on the outside looking in. I had assumed the perks would absolve me of my problems and issues, that success would just instantly make me 'happy'. It seems silly now – I was obviously still going to have good and bad days, though all of a sudden other people would see me as having no right to have a bad day – I had to be happy; I'd won.

A friend of mine, Henry Schofield recently married his long-term girlfriend Claudia, who works as a psychotherapist. I learned from her the necessity to stop looking for reasons in my own behaviour for other people's actions. I've come to realise that we are each responsible for our own actions and not for those of other people. Perhaps this is also connected with my anxiety-driven OCD and my constant battle to stop worrying about things that are out of my control.

My childhood household had been burdened by stress as a result of us constantly living outside our means. For less fortunate families like us it was like having our faces pushed up against a window, seeing what was on the other side for those who could afford it, with this invisible barrier between us. Yet we knew what really separated us from them was our finances (although, there is something in the invisible barrier – perhaps it's one we build ourselves with a sense of worthlessness). It was hard not to want material comforts – but I was taught early on that anything I wanted I'd have to work for. Not everyone took that approach. Entitlement issues exist at both ends of the spectrum. Those who have always had may feel they always deserve to have everything; those without may equally feel they deserve more but shouldn't have to do anything for it – both types are equally shit people.

When I had fewer responsibilities I was definitely more easy-going (or stupid) with my money. I was able to have a lot of fun, both by myself and with my friends, but that has made things harder for myself now. I still make money, but now I have more responsibilities I don't have the disposable income I did in the past. I've learned the important lesson that my money should never have been disposable in the first place. Is this is what being an adult is? Having to be sensible with the pennies so to take care of the pounds and to plan for the future? Now I have a wife, a mortgage and plans for children and most of what I earn goes towards our future.

I still talk how I talk, I still have the same mannerisms but I have the perspective of having seen both sides of the coin.

Now I realise it was a choice I made and I'm quite angry at myself for being as frivolous as I was when I did make any money. Much to Lewis's delight, I no longer frequent Selfridges, Harvey Nichols and Browns, nor do I pick up every tab any time I'm out and I don't keep up with the people who have a habit of going missing whenever a bill does arrive at the table.

I had to learn quickly about the pitfalls of success and how to deal with what other people expected from me. But with the success of my second album I was more secure in my work and I felt more firmly established than before – at least in my career. My personal life was still less stable.

Here's Lily joining me on stage in Brixton in 2010 after a shocking exit from the World Cup – still wearing our England jerseys from earlier in the day.

© Rufus Exton

Here's me hard at work on the set of the 'Just be Good to Green' video, wearing a watch kindly leant to me by my manager, Ged Malone. © *Rufus Exton*

© Rufus Exton

A pic of Ged (my manager) and me from Sonar – my first festival outside of the UK (*left*). Here's Felix getting the wrong end of the stick and the wedding photographer getting the wrong end of Felix as the rest of us mooned the people in the distance.

© Venetia Dearden

© Rufus Exton

The bird. How she puts up with me I'll never know, not least of all with me constantly taking pictures of her sleeping (which she does a lot) and posting them on Instagram. We both share a love for food – I noticed just how much during our first date when she made light work of a hot-dog.

© Rufus Exton

© Venetia Dearden

Millie and I eloped in September 2013 to Babington House in Somerset (*bottom*). With neither of us having time to swan off to Vegas for our Hen or Stag, we instead had a 'Hag-do' in London. Here we are on a bus with plastic-covered seating in-between venues (*top*).

© Rufus Exton

© Rufus Exton

My career is generally split in two – The Beats years and the post-Beats years. Following my first bit of chart success with 'I Need You Tonight', my career began to take off. Here I am winning a Mobo for Best Hip-Hop act (*top*) and trying to perform at Glastonbury – we kept overloading the generator, much to the delight of the crowd (*bottom*).

This was taken at the album launch party for *Alive Till I'm Dead*. Back row, from left to right: Thomas Jules, Maverick Sabre, DJ IQ, meI, Shereen Shabana, Ed Drewett, Katie Holmes, Oroh. Front row, from left to right: Drew Mclean, Ged Malone, Labrinth, Simon Burke-Kennedy, Alex Hayes/Cores.

© Rufus Exton

What a way to round off 2014! This was taken during the last show of the 'Growing up in Public' tour at the Camden Roundhouse.

© Ben Hughes

11. BREAKING THE ICE

Call me a cold-hearted cynic if you like, but I didn't believe that love at first sight existed. That was before I laid eyes on Millie. I remember the moment perfectly: I was in a newsagent around the time *At Your Inconvenience* came out and there she was, staring at me from the cover of December's *FHM* magazine. Lewis was there and he would testify that my face was a picture.

That was where it might have ended, but I overheard a conversation during a magazine photoshoot while we were rehearsing for the tour. One of the women from the magazine was talking to my publicist Phoebe about the reality TV show *Made In Chelsea*. I interrupted to ask them if they'd seen the one from the show who was on the cover of *FHM*. I hadn't seen the programme and I didn't know her name or that her family were half of the Rowntree Mackintosh Confectionery company but it turned out that Phoebe knew the editor of *FHM*, who knew Millie.

I joked, 'How come you haven't introduced us? I'm single, I thought we were friends!' and I forgot all about it. But Phoebe didn't. Phoebe's great. We stayed in contact even after she left Virgin and she's one of the true friends I've gained in recent years. She contacted her mate and that same evening I got a text from Phoebe: 'Here's Millie's number, she's expecting your call.' I called before I could bottle it.

I felt awkward as we began talking. I mean, I fancied her after seeing a picture on a magazine cover. What I didn't know until much later was that when I phoned Millie had been watching 'Just Be Good to Green' on YouTube and was trying to get it to pause before she answered. She had no idea about my music and had nearly been caught doing her homework.

Millie mentioned she'd just been watching David Attenborough's *Frozen Planet*. I happen to know a lot of polar bear facts for no particular reason and so, just because we didn't know each other well, a large part of our conversation explored my repertoire of random and useless information. Their skin is, in fact, black and their guard hairs, while appearing white, are actually translucent. They can run at 30 miles an hour. And how much does a polar bear weigh? Enough to break the ice with Millie, it seemed. Because, despite the slightly surreal chat, by the end of the conversation we had arranged to meet up. Thank god for David Attenborough and those cute-looking – but deadly – white, furry creatures.

We finally met in person on the last day of rehearsals for the tour, which also happened to be my birthday. I'd had a long hard day and so had she – she'd had to shoot a tricky scene for *Made In Chelsea* with an ex – and we decided to grab a bite to eat. So off to the Fulham Road I went in my brand new E Class to pick her up for a drive that took us to the Groucho. Millie said her impressions of me as I got out of the car to open the door for her were, Wow, he's tall and, What a lot of tattoos. My impression of Millie (after the *FHM* cover, I mean) was still along the lines of, She's fit. Her cut-class accent was quite a novelty and I'm sure there was lots about me that was unusual for her.

Neither of us knew much about the other and I think that helped us on our first date. Perhaps if we'd been more familiar it would have been more awkward, but once we got out of the confined space of the car we relaxed and flirted a lot and Millie says the main thing she remembers about that date was how much we laughed. Maybe that's also because we ended up getting quite pissed, although we had both vowed at the start that we weren't going to drink because we both had lots to do the next day. I told her she wasn't my normal type and she replied that I wasn't hers either – she normally went for the bad boys. Touché, point to Millie. I was even more interested after that exchange. Oh, and she clearly liked her food. She tucked into a hotdog rather than pushing a piece of lettuce around her plate and that won her points.

We had such a good time that I had to ring Felix to ask him to get a cab into town and pick me up. We were going on tour the next day and I didn't want to take a cab home tipsy and leave my nice new Merc stranded in a rip-off central London car park for days. Felix has been on more than one rescue mission for me, in the course of which he has got to know the streets and multi-storey car parks of Soho pretty well.

I left feeling things had gone well – a good end to an otherwise ordinary working birthday.

I had come off the tour and it was almost new year before I began to see Millie again. Our second date took place at the Dorchester hotel on Park Lane. Up in one of the rooms beforehand I had my hair cut and was getting ready. Millie was already waiting downstairs when I noticed a hole in the front of my shirt left by the safety pin in the dry-cleaning label and, much to Lewis's enjoyment, I was having a hissy fit. All a bit girly, I know, but I was trying to make an effort. I reluctantly tucked in my shirt and went downstairs.

Millie was in the China Tang bar with two lychee martinis – which also sounds a bit girly. And things only got better from there. When we went outside to have a smoke much later, Millie put me on the phone to her mum and – I'm sorry if your're reading this, George – I have to admit I was as pissed as a fart. And I can only hope I came across okay but I felt like talking to the mother was taking things a little bit fast... That said, I met Millie's parents, Nigel and Georgina – or George – in the flesh quite soon after we properly began our relationship, when they came to London to film a segment for *Made in Chelsea*. It was at a dog show and the family pugs Martha and Mable took a liking to me, so that was a win, but I think we were all quite nervous.

That day also marked the occasion of one of my very few brushes with *Made In Chelsea*. Millie was between seasons when we first met and at the pre-season catch-up meeting she told them she was seeing someone. The producers were keen to get me involved – in fact, it was probably a wet dream that one of their stars dated a rapper – but Millie wasn't having any of it and as a result she started becoming less involved in the show. The producers told her that if she did choose not to share then that would naturally limit her screen time but she didn't care. Neither of us wanted our relationship becoming part of *Made In Chelsea*.

Even so, right from the start we were both shocked and surprised at how much attention we got. On our first outing we got papped outside the Groucho, so either the photographer got lucky while waiting for someone else or was tipped off. Our first public outing as a couple was to the Brits and the press went pretty mad then as well. And so it began…

People often remark on how they see us as coming from different social classes – just as they latch on to the white rapper thing – probably just because it's much easier to gossip about the East End boy and West End girl, the pauper dating the princess, than it is to accept the reality of two people who met and are happy together. The first gig she came to was when I played at a club in west London and she had a prior engagement at a black-tie do that evening which she left early. So it's true we have come from different worlds but I think it was similarities as much as differences that attracted us. My nan always says that class isn't dictated by what you have in your pocket but by how you treat people and Millie and I share a lot of values. In any case, whatever differences there might have been soon faded, for the most part.

The only thing we don't have in common in our characters in a practical sense is that I can be quite the pessimist, while Millie is an incurable optimist. Having her around has helped me snap out of depressive periods while I have helped her rein it in a bit sometimes too. I often joke that Millie's world is pink and fluffy but in a world often so harsh and so cold it's refreshing to have her positivity around. We balance each other out.

From the minute her parents met me they were accepting,

kind and warm. I would have understood if they'd been worried by all of the things they might have heard in the media or read on the internet but they always took me for the person I was, standing before them, and judged me on how much their daughter loved me and how I treated her.

For her part, my nan was a bit nervous about meeting Millie, but only because it was a little out of her comfort zone. She maybe felt that someone so 'posh' might judge her for where she lived or what she did or didn't have, despite the previous advice she'd given to me. But none of those fears proved to have any grounding in reality and they're really close now.

With things going so promisingly with Millie I left for a tour down under in early 2012. When I'd been to Australia before it had been with Lily and Muse but now I was returning in my own right with my crew in tow. We played Future Music, a festival that toured the whole of the country, alongside Jessie J. On days off from festival dates I supported Jessie on her own tour. We got on like a house on fire – she was warm and welcoming, and I also knew some of her people already.

I was on one of my health kicks and it was a sober tour until we reached Adelaide for a festival date when we stayed at the hotel bar the night before the show until it closed. I ordered classic champagne cocktails for everyone. I don't like brandy or champagne alone but stick 'em in a glass together with a sugar cube and Angostura bitters and Bob's your uncle. A bunch of us took cocktails up to my room and then the others all went off to raid their mini-bars for a party that left us with about two hours' sleep before we had to get on the bus. My band were steaming but Jessie's crew got a bit more kip as they were on later. I made it to the stage and said to the audience,

'Everyone else in Australia has told me how shit Adelaide is...'
They got riled up. After a bit more lip from me and a bit of
back and forth with the crowd, the show started properly. And
it went off – it was probably the best gig of the tour.

On Jessie's own dates we played to easier crowds. They
weren't as varied as the festival audiences, they knew her
and most of them knew me since 'Read All About It' was a
huge success in Australia, though not every show was without
surprise. One night we went into 'Jungle' and before I knew
what was happening the stage was invaded by people dancing
in full-size animal costumes. A tiger danced over to me and
took off its head to reveal a smiling Jessie. She'd got me. But
even as I was laughing I was already thinking, I'm going to get
you back for this. I didn't have long to wait. My chance for
revenge came back in the UK the following month, when Jessie
played the Royal Albert Hall for the Teenage Cancer Trust and
we supported.

I was friendly with Jessie's hair stylist and we got her to get
a few extra Jessie J wigs. As soon as I finished my slot I got
changed and we were fitted with the wigs. It was a bit of an
uncomfortable experience, seeing myself with hair like that –
Professor Green as a woman. Fucking weird... really fucking
weird. Felix looked a bit too suited to his hairpiece. I couldn't
bear to look at him; it freaked me right out.

The Australian trip had an unexpectedly negative fallout
when it contributed to an argument with Chris Benns. I think
he had expected to come along but we couldn't afford to
have him come out only to have to fly home. What made the
situation worse was that he was in dispute with someone on
the management team. I had no idea about this until much
later because they didn't tell me and neither did he. All I

knew is that I'd reach out to him and he would only respond abruptly or not at all and eventually communication broke off entirely. I kept trying, just asking what was going on and saying that I hoped that he and his family were well. A year or so passed and by that time I knew that Chris had gone on to do well working back in fashion, but then I always knew he would as he's very talented. Eventually, he explained that he had intentionally been ignoring me and I snapped, not least because his problems were to do with management rather than me. I had put his absence down to his home life – I hadn't known about anything else. It wasn't until I later met a mutual friend, CK Lau from Christian Dior, that the friendship began to be healed.

CK Lau and I were discussing a suit I needed when he happened to mention that he'd seen Chris and we got on to the argument. That prompted me to send Chris a text and it turned out we were both in the same area of central London. That same day we called a truce over chicken wings at Busaba Eathai. We put it all to rest and realised it was just good to see each other again. We'd been proper idiots about it all and I'm glad we're cool now – although he is all too often busy being glamorous to hang out.

'Remedy' was due to be released from the album in the early summer and we made a promo t-shirt featuring an old-fashioned pharmacist's tonic bottle labelled 'Remedy'. Will Kemp, Rufus' best mate and Second Son business partner had designed all the merch. For an April Fool's Day joke, photo expert Rufus mocked up a bottle and filmed a convincing beer advert around it, my remedy for whatever ails you being a bottle of booze with the tag 'Don't worry 'bout tomorrow'. *The Sun* picked up on it and a brewery called Signature Brew asked if we wanted to make a beer for real. The answer to which was, obviously, fuck yeah, of course I want to make a beer.

The process was cool: I went with Rufus, Lewis, Ged and Simon from my management team and most of the regular crew to the brewery for a tasting. At first we sampled famous branded beers and lagers. We highlighted the ones we liked and the master brewer took notes. We came back six weeks later to find he'd come up with four different brews. From those four, after an intensive tasting process and much agonising between us judges, a winner emerged. The final tasting session happened during a tour on a day when I was so hungover that a beer was the last thing I wanted. But I thought, Hair of the dog it is, then, and got stuck in. The beer was launched at the same time as the single in June.

This was the time of Stone Roses mania, as the band were to stage their reunion shows at Heaton Park later that same month. Ian Brown had earlier contacted me about the gigs, his email coming as a surprise as we hadn't kept in contact since we talked about him guesting on my first album almost two years earlier. 'Sorry we didn't get to do that song,' he wrote. 'To make up for it, why don't you come and support us at one of the Heaton Park shows.' What the fuck? I thought as I read the note that came after midnight. I woke up Ged and my agent Alex as well – Heaton Park was going to be a big fucking deal. It was the Stone Roses' homecoming show, 16 years after the band had split up. Ever since, fans had wanted to see them one more time and the Roses received a Guinness World Record for selling all 220,000 tickets for the three nights in 68 minutes, the fastest-moving concert sales in UK music history.

I've performed at some impressive gigs in my time but if

I'm ever asked about what stands out for me, it's Heaton Park – though I wouldn't put it down to being my easiest crowd. On the night I was up, Liam Gallagher's Beady Eye were the main support and I was on before them. The act before me had left the stage to a smattering of polite applause but the audience weren't paying much attention and when I went on there were as many jeers as cheers. It was fucking frightening but not unexpected. From the moment I'd got that email from Ian I had been thinking about how volatile the 75,000-strong crowd was going to be. There were a lot of Mancs there and a lot of attitude. A lot of people were doing their first pill in ten years because they had two kids now, they'd got the babysitter and this was going to be a rare night off. They were in no way interested in Professor-fucking-Green when they had been waiting since 1996 to 'ave it with the best band that ever existed. They had no time for the southern rapping monkey about to pollute the speakers.

The crowd were fucking funny – scary, yes, but funny. They were all pulling faces – it reminded me of a saying about doing pills that came from Fat Daz who I'd met on tour with Plan B years earlier – 'you should have seen the fucking faces he was pulling'. Everyone looked identical – it was a sea of parkas, they all looked exactly how you would expect them to look at a Stone Roses gig. I thought, Ah, fuck... this is gonna be hard. We battled through a few tunes but I wasn't exactly winning. And then someone up front said something snarky that I could hear. I stopped the band, looked him in the eye and said: 'Sorry, what?' Then I looked up and said, more generally, 'There's always one cunt, 'int' there?'

And the whole of the park just erupted. Finally, some fucking response. They laughed and cheered. Turned out all I had to do was say the word 'cunt'. I wish I'd come out with it sooner. Quite surprised I hadn't. From then on, I had 'em onside.

Lily came on – as much a surprise to me as to the crowd; she'd taken a break from performing as she was preggers and she received an incredibly warm reception. By the time I did 'Read All About It' there were hands in the air everywhere. The band and I had done it. It meant the world to me because it hadn't been a given. If I hadn't got out there and shown them the lovely hairy pair of balls I've grown over the years it would have gone the opposite way. I would have had one of the most uncomfortable hours of my life and 75,000 people never would have contemplated liking a Professor Green song. I still haven't met Ian Brown, despite the email and the performance. I saw the Stone Roses take the stage that day but I had to leave for another gig before they finished. A moment missed, but hey-ho, I'm sure we'll bump into each other in the future!

Other standout live moments came in that same busy month with Radio 1's Live Lounge and the BBC's Big Weekend in Hackney. I love doing the Live Lounge. Everyone has to do one original song and one cover. I always forget the second part until the last minute and, given that I don't really sing, whenever I cover a song I have to write new verses so there's often a late night writing and arranging session before the recording. But this time there was too much going on in the run-up to the Big Weekend and, in addition, the BBC had invited kids from local schools to give them an insight into what goes on behind the scenes so they allowed me to perform an existing song due to its relevance in the shape of 'Hometown Glory', the Adele remix from *The Green EP* I'd released all those years before. I performed the track for Fearne Cotton, with IQ on the decks, with a small crowd made up of local students at BBC Radio 1's Hackney Academy. We went on to open the main stage at the Big Weekend with 'Jungle'. For once the opening line of the first verse, 'Welcome to Hackney,' was entirely fitting in the surroundings of Hackney Marshes (it's never quite the same when I deliver it in Skegness).

IQ had developed a habit of missing or 'forgetting' gigs and when it happened for the umpteenth time with a gig in Hertfordshire Lewis stepped out of his bedroom door and into the role of tour DJ. With both him and Felix on board it was as if our house-sharing setup had been completely transplanted into life on the road, although there were, as always, several complicating factors. One, Lewis hadn't been to bed the night before and so was shitting himself about playing out; two, I needed to be picked up from Plastician's wedding reception party somewhere in the middle of Oxfordshire, where things were getting rowdy. Skream was among the guests and was on good form and other musician friends such as Artwork and co were also there. Factor me in and it was basically like the Ghostbusters crossing the fucking streams to blast the shit out of the marshmallow man – a recipe for disaster, in other words.

Things were getting wild as I was getting ready to leave and I recall talk of large sums being bandied about to persuade me not to leave the party but somehow Lewis and Felix got me to Hertfordshire. I recall that Millie was in tow that night – she did a fantastic rendition of 'Jungle' in the car – and thanks to everyone involved (and copious amounts of vodka) the gig went well. Lewis went on to be indispensable behind the decks, particularly on the gigs when we only took the streamlined crew. He shares my cynical outlook on life and while I'd enjoy writing what a wanker he is I have to be honest – I love the fucker.

When it came to breaking for a summer holiday I made a return to Ibiza but it wasn't to be as easy as it had been the previous year. I wasn't on heavy-duty medication this time around but there were far more ups and downs. There was a different crowd and it felt a bit more of a restless household.

We'd come out to relax but Alex was constantly saying that there was work that needed to be done. He'd repeat it endlessly – he had to work, work had to be done. I'm all for hard work but there's a time and a place. He'd brought all his kit with him including his keyboard. But rather than keeping it in his room he set up on the outside table where everyone had to eat and drink. As we did our best to relax in the sunshine he wasn't only putting sounds together on the computer but he had his headphones clamped on and was tapping along, one hand on the table, beating out rhythms. It was like a nervous tic, endlessly drumming. It didn't make for a good atmosphere.

Everyone spoke to him about it, telling him that he was fucking up their vibe. So then Alex moved his gear inside the house. Not into his bedroom where at least it would have been out of the way, but just onto the table in the living room.

Early one morning we woke up to the sound of someone having sex nearby or at least that's what it sounded like. A rhythmic pounding of flesh on furniture. Bleary-eyed we left our beds and found Alex – bright and early, 6.45 am – in the living room, his foot thumping away on the floor, hard at work, headphones on.

It seemed like everyone was slightly more weighed down with concerns of one kind or another and that everyone was arguing during that second trip – even me with Millie, over absolutely nothing. Then Rufus drunkenly involved himself in our domestic and it took Rufus and I a long time to sort that one out. I guess we just didn't slow down as we had done the previous year. I remember Dream McLean took his first pill after I played Ibiza Rocks. I hadn't seen him for ages when he appeared with a silly neckerchief and round glasses looking like the fucking mixed race John Lennon. It took me a moment to realise that he wasn't quite right – having never done one before he was off his fucking noodle. It all got a bit much. The year before, when I'd been forced to be sober, had been much better. I got to wondering if all the partying was worth it in the end. Not just in Ibiza either, but generally. Yes, it can be fun but the pointless arguments that come with getting on it – the emotions, the comedowns – make for a heavy price tag.

Yet it was hard to avoid the big nights, particularly when I was out on the road. There were always drugs available as a touring musician. In September I went out with Guinness around Ireland on the same bill as Tinie Tempah and Example. As usual, there was all sorts to be had – I think people often see offering drugs as a way in to hanging out or getting to know me. I rarely take up the offer from people I don't know, but when promoters at a club offered me £500 and some goodies to walk into a Belfast venue it was a no-brainer – we took the goodies, turned my phone off and went to my hotel room and partied. Lost track of time and never ended up at the club.

I can't pinpoint exactly when I decided I wanted to ask Mills to marry me. Maybe Phoebe sowed a seed when she said, 'You're going to marry this one, aren't you?' Perhaps it made more of an impact coming from her because whenever I'd previously said I was serious about someone – and as she did my publicity I'd met a lot of people in Phoebe's company – she'd say, 'Yeah, yeah, you've still got one eye on the door...' so often that One-Eye-On-The-Door became her nickname for me.

I'd not seen strong examples of marriage when I was growing up and getting hitched had never been a top priority before. But now even Phoebe was saying that things were different with Millie. So maybe I can blame Phoebe, but if so I got my own back as I said the same thing about the man she is now engaged to.

Millie and I had been together a year or so and now I'd made up my mind – wherever the idea came from – I knew I had to do it properly and ask her parents. When we next spent a weekend at her parents' place in Bath it was torture from Friday to Sunday. Every time an opportunity arose to ask I was frustrated. I managed to corner her parents a few times but each time Millie would walk in. By Sunday afternoon I was a nervous wreck. I was running through scenarios in my head in which I was struggling to make up excuses to Millie that would allow me to disappear for the day and drive down to ask them again. It had to be in person; there could be no question of doing it over the phone. And I was basically at the point of starting the motor and waving goodbye when Mills announced she needed the bathroom.

I grabbed Nigel and George, hustled them inside and into the first room I could find. I had a fine speech I'd been building in my head for ages but the situation was almost paralysing and I simply blurted, 'This is the hardest thing I've ever done...' George immediately got the idea. She jumped on me and I didn't have to say any more. Then they both said, 'Yes,' which made things a lot less awkward. I just had time to show them the diamond that I'd spent ages tracking down before Millie came back. As we left Millie noticed George was crying at the window as she waved us off. 'God, she can be so emotional,' she said.

The next step was to get my nan and Millie's parents in the same room. I took everyone to the Hind's Head, Heston Blumenthal's pub restaurant in Bray for a meal together, a meal nearly spoiled by my nan – who also knew my intentions – appearing to be on the verge of giving the game away at every moment. There were a lot of dark, panicked looks going her way and a kick or two under the table as well. Millie's mum also looked very much as if she was having difficulty keeping the secret bottled up, but somehow Millie remained none the wiser. It had been over two weeks since I'd asked the Mackintoshes for her hand and I could tell the secret was weighing heavily on George. When I looked in her eyes, I could see it: Just ask her!

The next day we went to Paris.

Almost a year earlier Millie and I had gone to Paris for the first time together – it was thinking back to it that gave me my idea for the proposal. That first trip we had been invited by Riccardo Tisci at Givenchy to attend his menswear show and we travelled by Eurostar when we got chatting with a woman passenger. From what she was saying it sounded like her dad was an interesting guy and she kept referring to him doing long shows and things like that. Millie kept nudging my leg but I had absolutely no idea who we were speaking to. Our companion stepped out of the carriage for a moment and Mills told me we were talking to Stella McCartney. And I was like... Oh, right, I get it now. It probably would have clicked later when she began showing us ideas for the following season's sunglasses.

It was Stella who told us we shouldn't leave Paris without going to Lapérouse, a restaurant that she described as a Parisian institution. It had private rooms used by the old-school French politicians when they took their mistresses out. The women would be given diamonds as presents and, to ensure they were real, they would scratch the mirrors in the room with them. No scratch and it was fake – the bigger the scratch, the truer their man. That night, with a little bit of help from a model agency 'Next', we dined in one of the private rooms. I decided that this was where we should return on our second trip.

I had designed a ring myself (with a little bit of help from Dino at Frost of London) and the diamond was set in it. I packed, hoping to avoid the nightmare scenario of getting to Eurostar customs at St Pancras International only to be picked on by a jobsworth officer who would decide to search my stuff and turn up the ring in front of Millie. I was haunted by the idea until we were safely sitting on board the train. I'd been hiding the ring in Lewis' drawer. There were also a couple of sleepness nights when I nearly woke Millie from her sleep to ask her there and then – though I may have got a different answer if I did.

Millie thought we were going for another meeting with Riccardo. He was my favourite designer so my story that he wanted to see me about something didn't seem at all unlikely and it also easily accounted for any nervousness on my part. I had been very casual in inviting her along: you know, if you don't have anything better to do, Mills.

I filmed and took photos of Millie all day that day. I was surprised she didn't find it weird because, even after posting a YouTube channel and a Channel 4 show, as well as taking a million pictures on Instagram, I'm still not the best at documenting my private life. Despite that, I managed to keep up the subterfuge, even pretending to take several calls about the meeting during the day (thank you to my manager Simon, for listening to me chat nonsense down the phone).

We went back to the hotel before dinner and I planned that we should go for a drink or two to calm myself. But Millie took much longer to change than usual so I only had time for one to take the edge off. When we got to Lapérouse they gave us a room without a wall mirror, which threw a spanner in the works. By this time though, the pressure of the occasion had built up a bit too much and I'd had just about enough of waiting. The waiter had left and Millie already had her eyes on the menu. My friends had all said to wait until after the meal to do the deed, mainly for pragmatic reasons: otherwise, they warned, she'd spend all dinner ringing her family and friends – providing she said, 'Yes,' of course. But now I couldn't wait. I was too nervous. I knew I wouldn't be able to look at, let alone eat, my food. And so I left my chair got down on one knee and asked her to marry me almost as soon as we sat down at the table.

First she said, 'Don't be silly…' Then she saw the ring. She couldn't speak. It felt like an eternity had passed.

'You're going to have to say something soon,' I said. 'This is getting really awkward.'

And then she said it. 'Yes.'

We drank a toast as I sat down. When the waiter next came in, she showed him the ring, shouting, 'Look, I'm engaged!' and he couldn't have been more unimpressed. He was very French about it. I knew it couldn't have been the first time he'd seen someone newly engaged but even so, he could have pretended.

Millie did go on to spend the entire meal on the phone but I didn't mind; with the ring out of my pocket and on Millie's finger I could finally bloody relax! It was a perfect evening. We ended up back in the hotel where my memories get vague. One of my final images is of her almost scratching the enamel off the bath with her ring – making up for the lack of mirrors. Needless to say we had quite the hangover the next day. We woke the next morning and though nothing had really changed everything had: I'd taken a step towards marrying the person I wanted to spend the rest of my life with.

Despite losing my iPhone in the back of a cab and with it loads of new lyrics and voice notes, I arrived back in the UK wearing a huge smile but soon after the trip I suddenly had to put our plans on hold. And not just for the wedding – everything came to an abrupt halt when I was involved in an accident. It was May 2013 and there had just been a supermoon (a full moon when the Moon gets closest in its orbit to the Earth) in my star sign, Sagittarius. The last of these occurred almost four years to the day previously – 23 May 2009 – the day I was stabbed: there must be something in that which brings me misfortune.

I was at home, Lewis and Felix were living with us too. I'd had a gig the night before, so there were people littered around the house in states of inebriation and unconsciousness and I'd done the rounds to wake everyone up in preparation for a university ball that night. We'd organised two cars so people weren't all bunched up during the long drive. One had arrived and we were just waiting for the other. I went back out with my things and got an update from the driver. 'Two minutes,' he said. 'I'm just doing the paperwork for this car and by the time I'm finished the other one will be here'. So I left him to it and headed back to the house. I didn't make it to the pavement.

His car seemed to be parked but it was actually only in eco-mode. The driver absent-mindedly took his foot off the brake, the engine came to life as the car rolled forward and, panicking, the driver slammed his foot down on the brake. Except he'd got the wrong pedal. The powerful motor roared as it accelerated towards me. Almost in the same instant it hit,

I got my hands on the bonnet, hopping and trying to lift myself out of the way to avoid the impact. I almost made it, but my left leg was sandwiched between the moving car and one parked in front of it – my own, beautiful SLS. Having squashed my leg the car bounced back again. I hopped away from the impact and collapsed in the middle of the road, screaming in pain. I pulled my jeans up to see a massive dent in my leg. It looked very, very broken.

People in the house said it sounded like I had been shot. There was a bang, my scream and by the time Felix ran out, I was lying in the road. The driver walked over, crying, telling me how sorry he was. I didn't give a flying fuck how sorry he was! As rage came over me, the shock wore off, pain set in and it began to rain.

Thanks to Felix and a nurse who lived across the road, I was covered in a blanket by the time the first-response paramedic arrived. She gave me some gas – not the kind that my childhood dentist used, but the kind that makes you go all floaty and happy and with a dose the world became very pink and fluffy and also quite narrow. Not so fluffy, though, that I wasn't annoyed when my jeans were cut away (Acne denim isn't cheap). Then the ambulance arrived and, despite the circumstances, the ambulance staff asked for a picture. I was so fucked on gas and air I agreed. I even managed to Tweet and Instagram my plight, completely forgetting how severe things actually were.

An hour later and I was in a hospital bed in fucking agony. The first thing they had done on my arrival was to take the gas away. They couldn't give me anything until they worked out whether they needed to operate. I was immediately sent for an MRI scan on my pelvis. If I'd broken my pelvis I would have very quickly lost a lot of blood internally with no visible sign of what was going on. The danger was much more severe for me as I'm a haemophiliac. Fortunately, I'd managed to manoeuvre my pelvis out of the way in the split-second before the crash. I thank my lucky stars I did, because otherwise the injuries could have been life-changing. Life-ending. I don't really like to think about it.

By the time the tests were done, Dr Malik had arrived and arranged for me to transfer to a private hospital. Rather than wait to be transported I got Lewis to drive me and, eventually, with a little help from medication, I slept.

Discharged a few days later, I didn't know how I was going to cope at first. I couldn't get up the stairs – I couldn't do anything on my own. Millie and Simon helped me into bed and the recuperation began in earnest. Over the next couple of weeks or so I was massively doped up on painkillers. Codeine, tramadol and slow-release morphine were no light combination. I was having conversations with people who weren't even in the room, tripping out and having lucid dreams, and my whole body itched because of the tramadol. It got to the point where I couldn't do it any more. It was just fucking horrible, so I stopped taking all of it and I only allowed myself paracetamol. I was left with a dull, constant pain that was like a nastier version of toothache or an abcess (things I know a bit about).

The pain made me angry and I didn't want to take it out on anyone so I withdrew. Through all those times Millie was there; it couldn't have been easy for her. She showed strength when I was feeling overwhelmed and she helped me when it was really fucking difficult for us both. Her duties included changing my compression stockings all the while knowing that a wrong move caused me even more pain. Even her natural optimism was stretched. She must have felt like telling me just to cheer up a bit, but everything she did helped.

Along with whether or not I'd be walking up the aisle, another worry was my upcoming gig at Glastonbury. It was pretty much the first thing I thought about, even as I lay there in the road. I had been booked to play the Pyramid Stage and I didn't want to cancel or only manage a half-hearted performance. Performing on the main stage at Glastonbury came with a great deal of pressure even without being squashed in between two cars just a month before.

I'd also just recorded a song with Miles Kane, former Rascals frontman, called 'Are You Getting Enough?' and I knew he was also going to be at the festival. We got it out before Glasto and the plan was to perform it on stage together. The track had come about via Kid Harpoon (Tom) who had been introduced to me by A&R man Glyn. Tom didn't think the track would end up on Miles's album and so played it to me. A while after, we made some changes to the production, I recorded the lyrics and the track was done! Now everything seemed to be in jeopardy for my live appearance. But while Glastonbury was barely a month after the accident, I managed to get back on my feet in time. I wasn't all that steady, but I was standing (with the aid of a knee brace). I couldn't promise much for the dynamics of my show, but I was going to make it to the site and that was a triumph in itself.

Just a couple of days before the festival I talked to Miles and we realised that he was going to be playing the Other Stage at the same time, so that was the duet off the table. But I had other worries to occupy me when I got to Glastonbury. Even the path from campsite to stage was a trial. The first trouble I ran into – hobbled into, more like – was just staying upright on the uneven ground. At one point I was talking with Miles Leonard, who ran Parlophone, when I lost my footing and I couldn't put any weight on my left leg even with the brace. I went over backwards and my knee flexed so far back that my heel touched my arse. It felt like something snapped although, luckily, it didn't. Then I heard my post-gig TV interview on BBC Three had just been cancelled.

What the situation called for was Jack Daniels. Unfortunately, there was only brandy around. I fucking hate brandy. But this was a medical emergency and I drank a good part of a bottle before I went on. As the cocktail of brandy and painkillers began to make me feel pretty good, I took off my leg brace to begin the show. I was going to give it everything I had. Ged was shitting himself as he saw me risking my recovery by running around and jumping off the stage. I'd played warm-up gigs in the week before but I'd been much more cautious. Now I looked and felt like a different person, even though my knee eventually swelled up like a football.

As I came off stage there was a mate standing in the wings with a couple of treats in his hand. My work for the weekend was done so I put one in my mouth and off we went to party. It wasn't long before I was stopped by Helena, who handles my TV. 'Darling,' she said, 'are you ready for your interview?' The sun was going down, I was feeling woozy and BBC Three was back on. Oh dear. If I'd thought I was headed for live TV I would have walked right past my mate standing there with his hand out.

Helena told me to take my glasses off and examined my eyes. 'Oh, you look fine, darling,' she said. I looked around for my crutches and strapped up my leg in its brace again. 'Don't worry,' Helena said. 'We'll be straight in and out.'

She was being optimistic. We rode in a buggy for 20 minutes or more through the crowds of music fans to reach the BBC compound perched on top of a hill. 'Look after me!' I said to presenter Gemma Cairney as we arrived. It was nearly dark as I sat down, to be told that there were still 16 minutes of my earlier set left to play out on the telly. I've never liked hearing myself back and this was the last thing I wanted to watch, freezing cold and beginning to feel the effects. I was increasingly and unmistakeably high, but I began to think I might as well relax and enjoy myself. Gemma was lovely, as was everyone else on the crew.

Finally, the red light went on. As I talked, I watched myself in the TV monitors. I was feeling a tight, slightly sore, and stretched sensation across my forehead. The sight confirmed this was hot, red skin. 'Fuck, I'm proper sunburnt, aren't I?' I said as I watched myself taking the piss on the screens, which only prompted me to behave like even more of a moron, albeit a lovely one.

As the interview finished I was, given the circumstances, pretty proud of how well I held it together. I even hoped that viewers might think that anything out of the ordinary was just a result of the natural high from appearing on that big stage. But then I checked Twitter, saw '#glastogurn' and realised that wasn't the case… I later saw the producer of the show at another festival and she revealed that I'd entered the BBC's unofficial lexicon. 'Someone will radio ahead to let the crew know we've got trouble on our hands and we'll ask if it's a "Professor Green".' I said I felt bad about causing them difficulties. 'Oh, no, you were lovely,' she replied. 'You were the nice kind of trouble.' She said they had another name they used to warn of far worse behaviour – but she wouldn't tell me whose it was.

If I had a venue of my own I could have fun without quite so many people tuning in, an idea that once would have been far-fetched but began to be a real possibility as I looked into starting a club. I began talks with brothers Gerry and Jon Calabrese, owners of the Hoxton Pony bar in Shoreditch. We found a location for the new club at 1 Leicester Square in the West End. I contributed my name and plenty of ideas and between us we turned the fifth-floor venue into something which managed to capture the vibe and seediness of a tattoo shop that wouldn't look out of place in Gotham. Ink was the name. With exposed ceilings and ventilation, views of Leicester Square and VIP restrooms plastered with old pornography and Burlington toilets with high cisterns it looked the part.

With some hard work and PR we did actually get the club off the ground at the beginning of September. We had a launch party that went off with a bang but business wasn't as quick to build as we hoped, although we did eventually make a success of the nights. I found it a bit of a strain having to be there every week and it led to a lot of misbehaviour so, all in all, it was probably for the best when we found out the following January that the building's landlords had gone into liquidation due to a £600k hole we weren't made aware of at the time we shook hands. Add to that a chef who'd stolen artwork we'd kindly been lent and I had quite enough of my first encounter with the nightclub business. It was all a bit snaky for me – and that's coming from an ex-drug dealer. It wasn't all bad though – I met TV chef Gizzi Erskine when we booked her to DJ for the launch and we've been close friends ever since. And thankfully the stolen art didn't include any of the neon pieces by Chris Bracey, the artist I'd met at one of his own exhibitions. He'd kindly loaned us work from his Walthamstow studio and exhibition – God's Own Junkyard.

The launch of the ill-fated club was just a week before our wedding. Millie had been working hard all summer to organise the perfect day while I had my leg in plaster and was either in a bad place or trying to work on the increasingly delayed album. Because so much had happened during our short engagement we decided to join forces for our stag and hen dos. Neither of us fancied going away for a bender, either, so we decided to stay at home for one instead. We put out the invite to all of our friends, male and female, and the 'hag' was born.

We started the evening with with cocktails in the bar at Hawksmoor on Commercial Street where we ate our bodyweight in steak and then, in our one concession to traditional stag-and-hen cheesiness, got in a disgusting party bus with wipe-clean seats and terrible music. I shuddered to think about the shit that had gone on in there, but the bus served its purpose, both getting us to our final destination and getting the party started.

We drove to the Sanctum Hotel in Soho, where we had the two top-floor suites and a roof bar with a jacuzzi. And strippers. Millie and I left, slightly worse for wear, long before the party died. Everyone else carried on the rock-and-roll until the nearby Groucho club opened its doors for the day. I called Rufus from my bed at home later that day for feedback on the rest of the celebrations and he reported they were still at the Groucho drinking Old Fashioneds.

At last our wedding was held on 10th September at Babington House, a stately home in Somerset. We had a bit of a job finding suits to fit both best man Lewis at 6 feet 7 inches (or 8 inches if you believe him) and Rufus, who's more modestly sized. Millie's side of the church had more family than friends and I had more friends than family. My friends are also my family but it choked me that my mother and father weren't there. All the conflicting feelings about my dad's death came back to the surface.

Mills and George took care of many of the pre-wedding tasks and made a stunning job of it. I had joked with Mills that she was turning into bridezilla at times – though I was smart enough to help with the table plan to ensure that we separated the troublemakers for as long as we could.

For me the day became real when I slipped the knot on my tie, that precise second when I became ready. Then it hit me. Rufus enjoyed that particular moment as it was a rarity to see me quite that nervous. When we played on stage it was usually everyone else who had to battle anxiety.

After a couple of pre-ceremony drinks to settle the hands we all squeezed into a tiny chapel. There were far more of us than should have been allowed and it was lucky that Sue the vicar was, as she had told us, terrible at keeping count. The processional started and I heard the doors open but, as I was on the verge of crying, I thought it best to keep my eyes fixed straight ahead at the vicar. If I'd seen Millie crying I don't think I'd have been able to stop the waterworks. I had to ask Sue to tell me when to turn around and as she did I looked to see Millie at my side, trying to wipe the snot from her nose with her bouquet! George had passed her a tissue as she walked down the aisle but Nigel had grabbed the tissue and used it to wipe his own tears, a moment we all spent a lot of time laughing over when later watching the DVD.

Millie looked incredible. The heightened emotion, the months of planning and now Millie – my fiancé, my love –

was standing next to me and was about to become my wife. Nothing could spoil the moment, not even the snot she was trying to wipe with her bouquet.

At one point I managed to fluff my vows, much to the amusement of our guests. 'So what?' I said. 'It's not like I've done this before.'

We headed off to do the speeches but as we waited outside the doors to be introduced to all of our wedding guests – now stood where they were to be seated – ready to welcome us as husband and bride for the first time, my old friend Jonah ran up to me. 'Stephen! Stephen! I need a word.' My stomach sunk. What could possibly have happened? It turned out Michael – Chyna – had had one too many. He doesn't get out as much anymore as he now has two beautiful kids and the alcohol had got the better of him. He would later return on form.

My original stage name, OZ – which I had hoped had been consigned to the rubbish bin of history – made a reappearance in Lewis's speech. He subjected the guests, and this included the new in-laws as well as the old friends, to an OZ tune he'd recovered off an old hard disk. The bars stood up, fortunately, but the first raps I ever committed to tape were not what I'd been expecting to hear as we prepared to make the toasts.

It had been nerve-wracking writing my speech. I had only started the previous evening and finished earlier in the day, having first shared a draft with Rufus to get his thoughts. I picked out Ged and his wife, Eleanora, who I said had been like surrogate parents to me. I gave my love to my present family and, as well as thanking Millie, I thanked my nan, saying, 'When I was a child I found it hard, but as an adult I want you to know even if given the chance I wouldn't change a single thing. Being brought up by you and by Nanny Edie until she passed away and having Mark on hand, I was surrounded by people who loved me and had my best interests at heart and for that I'm truly lucky.

'I know it must have been frustrating watching me find my feet growing up, and having to put up with years of what you used to call talking music, all the thumping bass coming out of my bedroom, me wearing my trousers far too far beneath my waist and all the baggy clothes I've long since moved on from.

'Despite all of this you've always supported me and never had any doubts about whether or not I'd succeed. Even when I didn't believe in myself, you always did.'

I thanked Mark, too, for all the nappies he'd changed and being there for me all the way through – even to the point of helping me with my washing and dry-cleaning as a fully fledged adult. And I thanked Paul for being stern and yet always supportive. He'd understood what it was like not to have a father figure and he'd given me someone to admire. I also apologised to him specifically for the time my mates and I took his credit card to look at naughty websites, not realising that we'd entered into an ongoing subscription.

The rest of the day we were rushing around at a million miles an hour, but we did manage one picture in which the best men and I mooned the paps circling in the distance. Our official photographer was meant to get a snap of our faces as we did it but Felix pointed the wrong way and his hairy arse made an appearance in the wedding book.

And then the party started. It wasn't as debauched as the hag do (although Skream was on form and there was rather a lot of 8 per cent west country cider knocking about among the classier drinks) but it was an amazing night following a beautiful day. Jordan of the Rizzle Kicks was one of those who took the Babington House helicopter back to London after dawn, giving Lewis a lift too. It was Lewis' birthday – not a bad present, really.

The next morning I woke up in the bridal suite at the house, thinking how crazy it was to suddenly be a member of someone else's family and to have a new member of mine. Not to mention the beginning of a new family we'd started ourselves. The guests at our wedding had made it more special than I ever could have imagined. I felt the love and support of so many people. The 10th of September 2013 meant the world to me. Then Millie woke up and gasped, realising I was still in my wedding suit. I'd put her to bed a few hours prior... 'Didn't we?!'

13. GROWING UP IN PUBLIC

The honeymoon was blissful. We had two weeks to ourselves on the Amalfi coast and a couple of days in Capri in southern Italy. Autumn warmth, sunshine and privacy: we were barely recognised at all and we had lots of wine and pasta, wine and pasta, wine and… you get the picture. We had a quiet time until we bumped into Chris de Burgh and family in Capri and we all got a little merry. So merry that Chris decided he hadn't quite grown sick of singing the song he's best known for and repeatedly serenaded Mills with 'Lady in Red'. Fuck's sake. Nancy Dell'Olio, former girlfriend of Sven-Göran Eriksson, was also there and I noticed she was quite tactile as well – she reached across Millie to put a hand on my leg for a moment. Me a newly married man – and her about 20 years too late.

Back home the house that Millie and I had bought

continued to be renovated under the supervision of my uncle Paul. We lived in another rental with Lewis and Felix, the scene of the car accident, having moved out of Lots Road which had proved to be too expensive to keep up alongside all the mortgage and building costs.

Millie got on with running her fashion label and I got my head down on the third album. I'd meant to follow up on the previous one quickly, just as I had after the first album, but I'd spent a good portion of the year incapacitated, off my fucking feet and a little bit off my head too, what with all the painkillers. Now I wanted to get more material out as soon as I could.

I played a gig in Ireland and after flying back I went straight on to meet Millie at Ink. Around 2 am we got a cab home. We climbed the stairs to the front door and I remembered I'd left my keys inside. Millie's key wasn't working so I left her there with the bags and headed back in the direction of the downstairs gate. I was fiddling with her bunch of keys as I went when a hand grabbed my wrist and popped the clasp on my Rolex and tried to pull it off. But I pulled back on the watch and, before I even looked up, turned and shouted 'Run!'

I heard Millie run as I yanked on the watch but my back was to her so I didn't see which way she went. The tug-of-war over the Rolex continued with the mugger and the fight spilled out into the road when I heard Millie scream. I froze. What had happened? Was there someone else with the yout'? Had he got Millie? I needed to make sure she was safe. I let go of the watch, much to the surprise of the toe-rag who was trying to mug me. He made a run for it with the Rolex, stopping at the corner of the road to turn back and yell, 'I know who you are!

Where's your girl gone?' With that he flat footed it around the corner and disappeared.

I was still standing in the road, right next to Millie's car with her keys still in my hand. I got in and drove round the corner and into the next road, following the robber. I wound down the windows, all the while yelling Millie's name.

I heard her scream again. Now it sounded like she was behind me. I reversed, clipping the front light of a parked van. I stopped the car, got out, panicking and still shouting for Millie. Three passers-by, all young women, saw the fracas and called the police and, as they were doing so, Millie stumbled out of a front garden, hysterical but okay. She had only been screaming to try and get the attention of a neighbour.

I was relieved to see her but now felt all the anger about the robbery rising. I smashed the bunch of keys on the ground in a rage. I managed to find my phone, which I'd lost during the scuffle and tried to call someone local to find the little cunt who'd stolen my watch. I called everyone I could think of but no one answered. I knew Jon Calabrese was with Lewis and Felix and I filled him in by text. 'I've just been robbed for my watch on my own fucking doorstep'.

The police eventually arrived, opened the front door and took Millie inside. I was honest about what had happened, including using the car. They could have shown some discretion but instead they requested I do a breathalyser test. At which point I lost my temper and called them a name or two – perhaps not the best idea. I was restrained, cuffed and taken to the station.

By the time we got there I had calmed down and I took the test straight away, blowing the equivalent of a pint-and-a-half's alcohol in my blood. My hand was still bleeding from where I'd held on to the watch during the scuffle and I asked for both my hands to be washed and sterilised.

Ged had to be woken at home to organise me representation as I was to be questioned by the police. I was being treated – not for the first time – as a criminal rather than a victim. An emergency lawyer came out for the interview and I gave a no-comment to every question. I was going to wait to take legal advice from my own solicitor before I said anything, but the whole thing seemed unfair. I'd been the victim of the attack, I had tried to defend my wife and it was me who had been arrested, leaving a terrified and hysterical Millie alone. Not to mention the fact that I'd been robbed of my £40,000 watch. After the interview, they locked me up and I was left alone to think about what happened.

The press was full of POP STAR ARRESTED FOR DRINK DRIVING headlines and I expect many people assumed I'd rolled out of the club after an all-day bender, bottle of champagne in hand, and pinballed my sportscar from lamppost to lamppost all the way home. The truth was I'd had no intention of driving that night. I am not someone who would ever drink and drive. It's irresponsible and dangerous. I've got a string of parking tickets from leaving my car on the street overnight and Felix could testify to the number of times he has got out of bed to come and rescue me and my motor.

Millie found it hard to believe that I spent the whole of the rest of that night in the cells. She had never had any experience of the police system and it seemed to her obvious that the police were not acting fairly and that they wanted to make an example out of me. I was finally released at 9.45 am without having had a wink of sleep.

Later that day I was due on stage at BBC Radio 1's Teen

Awards. I'd got involved in the story of a teenage suicide survivor, a girl who'd tried to take her own life and thankfully not succeeded. During her recovery, on day release, she had seen someone else who was about to jump off a bridge and she spent two and a half hours talking him down, and she was to be recognised for her life-saving action at the awards. It was the fourth year that I had been on the panel and there was no way I was going to let her down. I fully intended to go.

The label and BBC Radio 1 were understanding of my situation but I wasn't about to shirk my responsibilities. I went home, showered and changed and went straight to the event at Wembley. Millie had friends looking after her. It was an important night for me – not enough is done to champion kids. Those in charge often let them down and that was something I felt particularly strongly that day. Then I received a phone call from Rob Hollaway at Mercedes. It had become second nature for me to start explaining what had happened and to be in apology mode from the beginning of every phone call but actually Rob only wanted to know that I was okay and that Millie was all right too. I really appreciated that touch of human kindness while all of this was going on.

A day or so later I went to give a statement under caution with my solicitor for the drink-driving but I refused to give the police a statement relating to the robbery. All I wanted to do was move on and protect my family. Yet my solicitor was later phoned by an officer who hadn't been at the scene but who nevertheless said that he didn't believe my version of events. His take on it was that I had faked the whole thing. I thought this sounded like the officer had a personal agenda and I saw immediately that it hardly promised an unbiased, impartial investigation.

I had to go back to the police station for bail. I still expected the incident would be quickly resolved, either through an NFA (no further action) or with a charge of drink-driving. If it was drink-driving – which I'd already admitted – I imagined I would be in court the following week, where I would plead that I drove under duress.

To my shock, I was instead re-arrested – by the same charming officer who had phoned my solicitor – for attempting to pervert the course of justice. I was told the police thought I had made up the theft in order to claim on the watch, they denied me a phone call and my house was searched under what was called 'section 18', which meant that anything they found – whether relating to the case or not – was admissible.

Felix was at home when they turned up and he wasn't allowed to leave their sight as they conducted a search for the watch they thought hadn't been stolen. He was treated to their snide comments as they rummaged through our belongings. 'Not all that, is it?' 'Where's the rapper's money?' 'Why has one woman got so many bags?' All that kind of thing.

According to the police officer back at the station, the three female witnesses said that Millie was in the car with me and we were arguing. But those girls had been a good hundred metres away and, anyway, I was in a Mercedes SLK, a car with low seats that make it difficult to identify occupants at any distance. It didn't seem credible. We weren't allowed to check the statements to see exactly what had been said. We were also not shown statements by officers on the scene that were said to conflict heavily with my version of events.

It wasn't until much later – the morning of the court case itself – that I would be shown the evidence against me. One of the girls had stated that she had seen me reversing the car;

all three had said they had heard me screaming Millie's name repeatedly and none had said anything about her being in the car. None of this I knew when I was faced with the new charge. All I was told was that the police wanted me to give up the defence that I had driven under duress. They would then drop the charge of perverting the course of justice – a much more serious offence that could see me in prison for at least a year.

Unaware of what the witnesses had really said, I couldn't understand why the police wanted to do this. It was a persecution purely – I could only assume – because of my reputation and because someone somewhere wanted to claim a big scalp. Either that or they weren't happy with someone from the wrong side of the tracks making good and inspiring anyone else to do the same. But how could I come clean? I'd already told the truth.

I was interviewed by the same copper who was pursuing this new line of inquiry. He questioned all aspects of my story, beginning from the moment I said we arrived home.

Why was I at the bottom of the stairs?

Because the top door Chubb lock wasn't working.

Was I even wearing a watch?

Yes, I was – the CCTV from my club clearly showed me being escorted out by security and getting into a cab with the Rolex on my wrist. The door staff said in their statement that I was wearing it.

Apart from anything else, the watch was new and not yet insured. It would have been absolutely pointless to fake its disappearance. Why claim I was robbed for a watch that wasn't insured and that I'd then never be able to wear again?

The copper pressed me. 'When the officers arrived on scene,

you said you went to find your wife. Now you're saying you were chasing after the attacker,' he said.

But chasing the robber and finding Millie were the same thing! Was he stupid? I had no idea where Millie went and the attacker's last words had been that he was going to get her. So chasing him was finding my wife and vice versa. Those were the answers I wanted to give the copper to show him what a fucking muppet he was being but I reluctantly kept my mouth closed, no commented, and allowed the time to pass... slowly.

A dark and difficult period began as we continued life with the court case hanging over our heads. Working on music helped me to get through it, although I had to force myself to get on and start writing. I was due in the studio the day after I had been re-arrested and I only went in because I knew that Chris Loco and Ina Wroldsen, a writer I'd wanted to work with for a while, were waiting. We worked on ideas for one track but we didn't get anywhere.

'Let's try something else,' I said and Chris played a sequence of chords that at last grabbed me. It was the song that became 'Lullaby'. During a break I'd told Ina about my idea for my next album, which had the working title of *The Blue Blanket*, after the blanket that Nanny Edie slept under, the one that I'd climb under every morning with her to read books, do puzzles or watch cartoons. Part of the idea was about missing that security – wanting to be told everything was going to be okay and being able to believe it like you would as a child. This was where I was again in my life as an adult, people telling me that things were going to be okay and that I was going to come out the other side. I was old enough to know that I might not.

I took a break while working with Ina on the lyrics at one point and wandered back into the studio just as she was singing the chorus that was still lacking a final line. I waited for her to finish before opening the door and as I was stood there the words 'Can you sing me your last lullaby' came out of my mouth. I felt stronger for having come to the studio and written about facing adversity. It helped to strengthen my resolve to battle on – and I was going to need all my resources.

The court case was much delayed, each new setback adding to our frustrations, and the newspapers did their bit to make things worse, making up claims and curiously seeming to know exactly when to be outside the police station to take photos of me when I was being charged. Press interest in my life was nothing new. I've often been the subject of fabricated stories – 'suicidal thoughts' or shit like that. Despite never trying to exploit my relationship with Millie to make money, the papers seem fascinated by the tiniest detail. My publicist even got a call from one of the red-tops requesting confirmation that we'd missed a London fashion week dinner because we'd stayed up too late at the Groucho the night before – scandal! At least there was some truth in that article and usually I wasn't that bothered by the media. But there was something about the way the media zeroed in on the drink-driving – rather than the robbery – that got to me. The coverage seemed to go on and on, particularly when the trial date was postponed. People kept talking shit and someone even published my address as part of a story. The bad publicity began to affect my career. I'd been working with Puma to design my third collection of clothes and they severed the connection without even so much as a conversation. It's a shame – I've no doubt that if Lisa at Puma hadn't been on maternity leave the outcome would have been different as we had a brilliant relationship with her after all the years we'd collaborated. An endorsement deal with Pepsi disappeared and the Remedy beer was dropped by major stockists.

I was eventually charged. The CPS decided to drop the charge of perverting the course of justice and my friend the DC unsuccessfully contested the decision. I was told when I arrived for charging that there was a discrepancy with the CPS decision. My lawyer explained this was impossible; it was always very black-and-white and this was the DC engaging in more bullyboy tactics to wring out his last bit of enjoyment, knowing I'd be at home anxious for another night, waiting for their decision.

Eventually we got to court in March. A top barrister had offered to take my case for free because of the work I'd been doing promoting awareness of depression and suicide, something that had affected his life. Unfortunately, he was on another case and the judge wouldn't allow him out of court to deal with mine. We tried to change the date but were given a stern 'No'.

When we arrived for the hearing we got to see the police statements for the first time, alongside the witnesses' evidence. In my own statement I mentioned the cuts I sustained on my hand as part of the tussle, yet all the police statements – dated days earlier – specifically claimed that I had no such injuries. But how had they known in advance what I was going to use as part of my defence? All six of them seemed to be contradicting something that, according to the date of their written testimonies, had not yet been said.

In a further attempt to undermine my case, the police stated there were no cameras on the route the robber had taken and so no images could be produced in court. My lawyer visited a college on the road and was told not only that they had CCTV but that there was footage of a man in a hoodie getting into a car at the time in question. The college authorities said that they could only release the tape to the police. The police responded that nothing relevant had been recorded and denied us access to the material. I would have cried if I wasn't so vexed. I pleaded guilty to drink-driving and hoped the court would show some leniency but they took away my licence for a year.

You might not think it from the comment I gave as I left court – 'The only people wasting police time were the police' – but I know they're vital in some aspects for society although there's a lot of truth in what I said about my own case. There are many good coppers out there doing a great job for the right reasons. Yet while I have talked about being on the wrong side of the law myself, I've also been a victim of serious crime who has been let down. The police have never been effective or trustworthy in my experience. I end up sympathising with the large numbers of people who don't feel like they can trust the police either. They can't.

I was branded a liar and the worst of it was I hadn't even been able to call Millie to give a statement in support. We had worried that if she corroborated my story they might demolish her credibility as a witness or even arrest her for perverting the course of justice too. Everyone had told us that the first year of marriage can be hard but we hadn't expected anything like this. Ever optimistic, Millie said, 'Whatever doesn't kill you makes you stronger,' and together we got through it. I continued to work and began writing again. As the music materialised I felt a great sense of relief.

There were some lighter musical moments too, like the verse

I contributed to Meridian Dan's 'German Whip' remix that came out in April. It included the line 'Swear down I could have sworn I just saw Brian Harvey in a car with suicide doors', a nod both to the frontman of East 17, the band I'd loved as a kid, and to the incident in 2005 when he managed to accidentally run himself over in his own car after eating one too many baked potatoes with cheese. At the time he said he'd tried to open the door to be sick and somehow fell under the wheels when the car rolled forward. Brian must have heard the Meridan Dan track because later that year he posted a totally bizarre clip of himself doing a parody of the song. You can see him in his YouTube film, rapping along to the track while writhing on the ground next to a car and waving potatoes and cheese around. But as a big East 17 fan, I really hadn't been going after him like that – it was all in jest. I also managed to run over Katie Hopkins in the same lyric, which was due to be used on the main radio version – in fact it was, until the whole palaver over my drink-driving conviction and then my contribution was no longer broadcast.

When it came to finishing my own album, the court judgement continued to have an effect on the way I worked, if only by making the writing and recording process slightly less spontaneous. Naughty Boy would phone me at 11 or 12 at night and say, 'Come to the studio,' and, not having my driving licence for the year, I'd have to start arranging transport. But minor annoyances aside we at last got through the much delayed collection of songs, working with Chris Loco (who also produced 'Shadow of the Sun', my favourite song on the album), Mojam, Kid Harpoon, Cores and others.

In the studio nowadays I usually work from memory. Writing for someone else to perform is pretty much the only time I put things down on paper. For me it's easier to get behind the mic with my first four bars and build from there, recording bars as I come up with them and freeing up important space in that brain of mine.

It was great to work with Lily again in some capacity. She wrote the chorus to 'Can't Dance Without You' but her vocal didn't end up on the final version. I wish she'd stayed on it: it was a bloody headache trying to find someone to bring the charm she did to it. A lot had happened in both of our lives since we'd first known each other – we've both married and settled down and we haven't had the chance to jam as much as we once did. Lil moved to the country with Sam and has two wonderful children.

I'd had the title *Growing up in Public* in mind for ages and somehow, with everything that had happened, it had become something of a self-fulfilling prophecy – it had a hell of a lot more meaning for me than it had two years earlier when I first thought of it. We made a spoof *Hello!* magazine-style video promo for the album featuring me and Mills in a rather nouveau riche mansion – me mowing the lawn and cleaning the pool, Millie just being glamorous – as a way of making fun of the press interest in our private life. I was in tears of laughter when I saw the final cut. A lot of people who saw it probably thought that it was real, which only made it funnier.

I got talking to Neon artist Chris Bracey at his latest exhibition on sexualising religion and mentioned 'I Need Church', a song I'd just finished for the album. He said he'd never done a record cover and I invited him down to the studio I shared with Alex to hear the music and said if he was into it we should collaborate on the artwork. He loved what he heard and the rest, with his red neon, gun-toting Jesus, was history. Sadly, Chris passed away in November 2014 – lost to prostate cancer. He was a lovely bloke and I was lucky to work with him. He was a proper gent and he made a huge contribution to my album – I often think about him and the conversations we had, as a piece of his art is the first thing you see in my home, reflected by a mirror when you enter the living room.

'Lullaby' was the lead single, and you know what, the public responded to it. I think some outlets were reluctant, but I have to thank all the good friends I've made in the industry through the years for taking that record and giving it airtime. The music business moves quickly and fans consume music very differently nowadays. Even though I had barely been away it felt like another comeback. And it was a big fuck-you to everyone who'd doubted whether or not it was going to happen for me this time round. There were a lot of people glad to have me back. I'll always be thankful to those who stuck by me in those times, to the people who loved that song.

Tori Kelly, who featured on 'Lullaby', did more promo with me than any other artist I've worked with and that was despite living in California – her vocal performance was insane, not only on the track itself but also every time we performed it, on stage or in a studio. She was a new artist signed to Capital in the USA and managed by Scooter Braun, whose other clients include Justin Bieber. Tori was a sweetheart and has been doing huge things in the USA. She moved in a good circle, too. So far I've met her mum, dad and bro as well as Claire who looks after her – she's in good hands.

When I finally got to move into my new house with Millie that meant it was time for Lewis and Felix, our surrogate children (one is older than me), to spread their wings and fly. Our unit had developed a family vibe, something solid, over the three years we'd shared homes and it had seen us all through some crazy times. We had shared a lot of good times.

There was one party at which even I will admit I went a bit too far – I misjudged how much I'd had to drink and was found upstairs slightly unresponsive (I reckon I just needed a nap). Millie shouted for Lewis and Felix and before I knew it I was in a private hospital on a drip. When I came round I was fine and I didn't really understand the concern. I felt lovely and hydrated but I could tell by the faces around me that they were quite unimpressed. The nurses ran a few tests and I was discharged the following morning and the hospital bill following in the post a few days later. That little jaunt came in at over four grand, Mills having made the decision to take me to a private hospital to avoid ending up in the papers. Another costly medical misadventure.

Our shared house saw one final celebration before we left – and a long, hard and impromptu one at that. That night we had all been out separately and arrived home not at all late and we could easily have left it there. Or rather, any other three people might have left it there. This time it was Felix, usually the smart, level-headed, on-the-ball one, who instigated the party. Flash-forward to the early hours and we were still going round the kitchen table and suddenly it seemed like the best idea in the world would be to get Millie involved in the send off – after all, she'd been an integral part of the household too. Felix woke her up and she wasn't too impressed although I think she appreciated the sentiment. When the moment came to move, it was hard for both Millie and me watching Felix and Lewis pack up their van and leave, even though it was only half an hour down the road.

14. Full Circle

The 'Growing Up in Public' tour was postponed twice because of all the palaver that led to the album being delayed and I really didn't know what sort of reaction to expect when we started out at the end of November. If I'm honest, I didn't go into it with any positivity and was prepared for the worst. Would all the fans still turn up? As it just so happened, everyone did. And some.

We made some changes to the band and got everything sounding bigger than it had before. Guitarist Louie's brother Ricky came on board as musical director and worked his magic. One constant was Katie Holmes, a vocalist brought on board by my old MD, Oroh. Katie and I both geek out over house renovation and often do double dates with our partners. She's become like an older sister, a sister who's a lot older. Like, really old. (Only joking Katie.) She has as much to do with the success of the live show as I do. I've been a support act for alot of artists and in turn I've had the likes of Ed Drewett, Wretch 32, Rizzle Kicks support me, and even Ed Sheeran on a mini-Irish tour. Not much chance of Ed ever supporting again – not when he can sell-out three Wembley Stadium gigs. I still remember him telling me quite clearly what he wanted to achieve and it's been amazing seeing him make such light work of it. Rather than another act, we asked IQ if he fancied opening up.

I was on better form than I had been for a long time. A lot of artists find touring the hardest part of the business but I love it – being on the road might be a fucked-up routine but at least it's a routine of sorts and humans don't function well without routine. IQ also made a return to form – I'm not sure I'd ever seen him so well – his sobriety put me to shame! The response to songs both old and new restored the faith I'd lost in myself – it was good to get out and see some familiar faces along with a bunch of new ones.

Behind the scenes we got right back into the swing of things together. There were a lot of highs and there were a lot of highs and there was also a few lows – or rather, those moods where you become susceptible to emotion after too many late nights. It was an emotional tour, not only because IQ was along again; Rufus was also back after an absence. It was the old firm again with the exception of Thomas Jules and Cores. All the good chemistry made for good vibes on stage and as we headed towards the homecoming finale gig in London, it began to build into a crescendo.

After playing our Manchester gig we went to a club to see Giggs do a show and as a result got to Birmingham the next day after a pretty sleepless night. I saw Millie for the first time on tour at Birmingham, where she was in town at the Clothes Show with her collection. The city has consistently been one of the best crowds for us – with all the energy they put in, I have to give it back and it's always an exhausting gig. This one wasn't helped by a pre-match warm up at the Malmaison Hotel, as I drunkenly explained to the Birmingham crowd, asking them to forgive me while I took a seat for a moment on one of the monitors, much to the dismay of my wife. To the delight of the band, Millie came along with a few of the models from her show.

I slept like a baby that night, leaving me in better shape for a slightly more conservative gig at Norwich, after which we had to make it back to London for a charity do at Downing Street. On the road I probably get, on average, the contents of a full night's sleep every three nights of performing so I arrived at Downing Street feeling slightly worse for wear. The reception was in the Chancellor's official residence at No 11, put on by the Starlight Foundation for kids with very severe or terminal illnesses. There were loads of stars from TV, sport and music and a wildlife expert with some exotic animals, as well as the incredible kids themselves. There was a particularly special little girl called Ellie. She had a condition that was so rare they were thinking of naming it after her and in the course of her life she'd had scores of operations. She was such a little ray of sunshine you wouldn't have believed anything was wrong.

I'd gone to Downing Street to cheer the kids up but they'd cheered me up instead, as had the sight of seeing our security manager Trevor's arsehole flap for the first time – at the sight of one of the other guests, an albino snake. I also managed to get peed on by some weird creature the kids had been allowed to meet. And I met McBusted. I fan-girled a little bit.

Then it was off to Bristol where I saw Millie for the second and final time that tour and she brought along her parents (which was fun but made me realise how much I swore on stage and how incapable I was of stopping it). The penultimate gig of the tour was Bournemouth, which Dream Mclean and I followed up with sandwiches, pints of lemonade and watching *The Purge: Anarchy* in preparation for London – a homecoming gig at the Roundhouse in Camden.

I woke up on the morning of the show buzzing with nervous energy and full of anticipation. The last show we'd done in London was at the larger Brixton Academy to an over-capacity audience which went berserk. The Roundhouse had a lot to live up to. Ellie from Starlight and her mum came to see the soundcheck: we figured that her staying for the whole show might be a bit late and this way she got to hear some songs in a practically private performance as well as meet Rizzle Kicks, Miles Kane, Millie and the band. After we said goodbye to Ellie, we went on to a pre-match dinner at notorious Chalk Farm pub The Stag, which not only exceeded the three-pint rule but turned into an after-party – before the show had even started.

Back at the Roundhouse, I stepped out on stage to the warmest of receptions and any anxiety I might have had quickly disappeared as we got down to business. The floor heaved, everyone in the circle was out of their seats and the roars from the crowd were deafening. Rizzle Kicks and I got to perform 'Name in Lights' from the third album for the first time and, with most of my lot in attendance, there was a larger than normal stage invasion during the Kamo and Krooked remix of 'Monster' that we worked into the set. Rizzle Kicks weren't the only guests that night though...

'Read All About It' will always remain very dear to me, even if it's so tied to me that I have been known to call it the song that won't fuck off. Sometimes, when everything goes right, the song brings back all the emotions that I felt when I first wrote it. I launched into it at the Roundhouse during the encore, expecting to hear Katie, who usually sings it with me, in my earpiece. Instead I heard another very familiar voice. It was Emeli. I hadn't counted on her making it to the London show. I knew she had a lot on her plate and I hadn't seen her when we first left the stage. I stopped the band to give her a hug. I forgot how much fun it was performing together. The track was such a pivotal point in both of our careers and meant a lot to us both. The crowd definitely fed off and into our energy; I'd really missed being on stage with her.

All the emotion came flooding back. I felt that sadness and regret about my dad, mixed with defiance in the face of adversity. Millie and my nan were up on the balcony, along with the rest of my friends and family. So many people I loved up there were supporting me as I performed the song to a crowd of thousands, all singing the words right back to me. What with everything that had happened that year I just hadn't counted on the success of the tour. The gig couldn't have ended any better.

After the show I put my sober face on – at least until Nan had left. Lulu was there too, which my Nan obviously loved. 'I bet you don't even know who I am,' Lulu joked. I went into a line of 'Relight My Fire', cringed inwardly slightly and stopped. The after-party started – or rather continued – in the bar and went on for days back at our house as the perfect conclusion to the year.

Yet certain sections of the press ignored the good stuff and went right on running stories on me, as they have done ever since I got together with Millie. It seemed like they were always looking for bad things or turning innocuous moments into dramas. You wouldn't think I had found any kind of happiness if you believed everything you read. Of course, I know that good news isn't what the gossip pages want. It's a good thing the headlines don't have to be factual: 'Millie and the Prof have a night in, cook, eat food, wash up, cuddle the dog on the sofa and then go to bed without having sex because they opted for a *Game of Thrones* marathon instead'. Not really what they're after is it?

I doubt they'd be interested in knowing what really happens. The time I told her I hadn't managed to buy her a birthday present, I got her picked up without any idea where she was going and dropped off at China Tang, the bar at the Dorchester where we had our first proper date, and she arrived to find me sitting there with two Lychee Martinis – her glass with a diamond bracelet around the stem (she nearly finished her drink before she noticed it!). Another birthday I told her I'd booked us economy seats to New York and couldn't get a room in the Standard Hotel when we then flew first-class, stayed in a corner suite at the Standard and had one of the most special dinners at Morimoto. The sous chef Rob made everything in front of us fresh before he served it – all Omakase. I have to thank Goldie for the hook-up! I also surprised her with a watch. Another time we did argue a lot. We took a last-minute holiday in Jamaica and as well as getting a tan we decided to detox – no alcohol, no sugar, no carbs. It was awful. We hated each other, or thought we did, for the best part of two weeks. Eventually, we decided to eat normally and, suddenly, everything was brilliant again.

And then there was the first night spent in our new house. We turned up at the front door with just a mattress in the back of the car, took it inside and slept on it. There weren't even curtains up yet, so we just chucked the mattress on the floor, lay on it under a duvet and watched the dawn and the sun come up. Special times, but I'll admit that the papers aren't going to hold the front page for them. That said, they've poked their noses into almost everything else over the last couple of years. Even my dogs have become well-known, particularly Alfie.

Despite all the intrusion from the press, the love I received when I got back to playing live was unparalleled; it's incredible to have fans who are that supportive in such a fickle industry. It's funny, all the things that used to niggle at me have become a lot less irritating now I don't pay them any attention, particularly now I have finally found contentment in my personal life. I have clear goals for the future and that makes them a lot easier to work towards.

Maybe the reason that some people have a hard time believing I'm happy is that, until recently, I've had a hard time believing it myself. Depression marked my family life and my outlook on the world. From my dad's struggle with his demons to my own periods of darkness, it's been a constant presence throughout my life. Writing has always been an outlet for me, a way of making sense of the jumble in my head and to stop thoughts racing out of control, but it's not always quite enough.

I'm trying to understand depression – especially as it affects young men – in the hope I can make some difference. It's very easy for people, once they become a celebrity, to say fuck-all or shy away from big issues. But now I'm feeling more comfortable in my own skin – as well as recognising, however reluctantly, that I'm a proper adult now – I've been trying to be more active in fighting depression.

Mental health is not a glamorous or sexy area but I think back to my childhood and how it might have helped if I'd known more about it. If there had been something to read, or someone I could look up to who could have showed me that, although I didn't have a mum or a dad living with me, I had what I needed. I could have done with an example to show me that successful, happy people didn't always come from perfect families and privileged backgrounds – that things would always change, that they keep on changing and that my life wouldn't always be the way it was. Society pressures us all into believing that if we're not happy all the time then there's something wrong with us. But I've come to learn that happiness isn't a permanent state and – here's the key – neither is sadness. I wish my dad had known that.

I've come to realise that the simple fact of speaking out is important. If I can help others who come from disadvantaged backgrounds to believe they can do more than society thinks is right for them, then I'm all for it. I still receive a lot of backhanded compliments but, you know – low expectations are easy to exceed.

Becoming more outspoken about depression and male suicide in particular has led me to me becoming a patron of the charity CALM (Campaign Against Living Miserably) and making documentaries with BBC Radio 1 and more recently BBC3. I've met other people whose lives have been affected by suicide or who have attempted it themselves.

It's also meant I have found out more about my father. Long ago I stopped trying to guess what was going through his head but there are so many other questions for me. I wish I'd had more time to speak to him as an adult, to understand more about him and his upbringing. The producers of the BBC3 documentary reached out to his friends and relatives, people I hadn't seen since the funeral. And it was gruelling. Talking about his suicide or my depression isn't easy at any time, let alone in front of a camera. Learning things about him for the first time stirred up my emotions for all to see – but, as frightening as it was for the world to see me during such lows, I hope my experience encourages more males to be more open and honest about their mental wellbeing.

I discovered that Dad's brother, my namesake Stephen, had died a year and a half before my birth, leaving behind his parents and siblings but also a daughter, who sadly passed away before the age of 20. Three brothers, two hanged, all dead. I specifically asked for a therapist to be involved in the radio documentary to give a professional point of view and his words made a great deal of sense. He said that humans are resilient and we puff our chests out and survive 99 per cent of what's thrown at us. But surviving something doesn't mean you've dealt with it and the truth is that we're not designed to carry on unaffected. When you lose someone, that grieving never goes away. Those emotions are under the surface, ready to flood back. I want to keep on learning so I can get closer to my dad and don't go on to pass the same repressed emotions on to the next generation.

Working on these programmes brought stuff to the surface that was so deeply buried I didn't even know it was still there. I broke down many times and I was left with emotions swimming about the surface. When everyone else on the crew went home for the night and left their work behind them, I was still living it. I had been so busy before that I'd never dealt with a lot of these feelings but they began to fill my days. If I don't seem on best form during the documentary it's because I wasn't – the days were long and exhausting and the nights were sleepless, my familiar friend anxiety finding home where it always has, leaving me feeling frantic.

There was some light in what I learned. We went to the Maytree Centre, a charity with a house for suicidal people but not the grim institution you might imagine – no straitjackets, iron bars and locked doors. Maytree provides sanctuary for people at the brink of ending their lives. Residents stay for just five days but very few of those who have gone there have ended up committing suicide. Yet Maytree is the only place of its kind in the UK.

Making the documentaries pushed me out of my comfort zone, made me think about my own past and I have vowed to resolve issues that I have long not dealt with. I used to think that I could shut down difficult relationships but now I realise I have just left loose ends. It doesn't do anyone any good and I even made up my mind – very recently – to phone my mum. It was good to hear her voice. I've never not loved her, it was just that in breaking off contact I made a decision I felt I needed to at the time. It can be so easy to avoid difficult conversations but adulthood has taught me the easiest way to find peace is by resolving to the best of my ability everything I have the power to.

These new areas of interest are very different to the kind of things that used to keep me busy but I know that life isn't always going to be as exciting as it was in the past. I can't keep expecting to write so intensively about what's going on. Sample subjects from the last 18 months might include how terrible Farrow & Ball paint is; learning to put my boxers in the washing basket because otherwise Millie gets pissed off; forgetting to pay the cleaner and stressing over the potential rise in interest rates.

I guess these are things a lot of people can relate to but they might not make for very exciting music. Still, I do actually hope that life is calming down: boring, in a lot of ways, is good. Although I continue to accumulate tattoos – most recently on my head. (Millie was at her parents' and the famous tattoo artist Cally-Jo was in town, so why not? Millie then went on holiday without me again when she went to LA for the Coachella festival so I got an old tyme bulldog puppy and named him Arthur – not sure how I can, or if I should, exceed these.) Now I've finally moved into my own house I have the space I need to unleash my creativity again. After so much time hanging out and working in clubs, I'm enjoying being at home. But just because I'm married and I have grown up a bit doesn't mean I'm less relevant as an artist. I'll always be that guy those things happened to and I will always draw on those experiences, but they don't define me – I won't let them.

At the moment I'm taking back control of what I do. With a better, healthier head on my shoulders I've returned to being the pro-active me and it's been a welcome return to form – for everyone else as much as for myself. I've been sitting down with Rufus to decide where we go next as, along with Lewis and Felix, we plan world domination. It's refreshing. I've achieved so much but at the same time with all the change it feels as though I'm starting again. Everything's changed. I did a few university freshers' gigs recently – a PA tour of some big student towns – and some of them were the sickest nights of late. Club venues with people packed shoulder to shoulder, jumping, screaming and some eventually making it over the barriers. There's something rewarding about sweat dripping off the ceiling. And it isn't only club gigs where that can happen – we've had that every time we've played Birmingham Academy and that's a 3,500-person room.

The greatest thing about my shows and getting out on the road is that the fans know the music so well. I see people at every gig who can sing all my songs word for word. Not just the catchy choruses, but more importantly the verses too. As annoying as my voice may be to some it has a distinct clarity which I'm lucky to possess. I can engage the whole crowd and address everyone but for some reason – and I don't know why – I usually make a connection with a handful of people that I perform to in particular.

'Read All About It' still makes a huge impact on any audience. But it once made a very different impression when I performed it after 'Where Do We Go?', the last lines of which run: "'Cos I've got a girl and you've got a man but I'm wondering what if... ?' But this time I got the 'man' and the 'girl' the wrong way around. Even the hardcore fans in the front row didn't notice but as we launched into 'Read All About It', I collapsed in laughter. I couldn't carry on. I had to explain what had just happened to the crowd. But when we finally got into 'Read All About It' the energy was all the stronger for it – despite its inspiration it isn't defeatist in the slightest; it's about having the bollocks to carry on.

That performance was a reminder that I like things to be unpredictable. As a fan myself, I hate it when I go and see someone play and I can tell there's zero difference between what I'm seeing, what they did the night before and what they're going to do tomorrow. Interaction with the crowd, the spontaneous shit, that's what it's all about. Keeping a live connection with everyone who is listening to the music.

I feel good: even after being crushed by a car, being nicked myself after having my watch stolen and through all the setbacks and tribulations over the years. Writing about everything in this book has been one of the scariest tasks I've ever undertaken. It's hard knowing whether or not stories so personal will strike a nerve with anyone reading this but it's been a wonderful opportunity to revisit times past and to relight a part of myself, encouraging me to get back in the bloody studio and get on with what I'm good at.

I've been extremely fortunate to come so far in an industry where most never do and it's important I don't squander that. I used to be scared to say I'm happy, always cautious of what might be around the corner, but fuck it; I've achieved things important to me and there was no point in all the hard work if I can't honestly say I've enjoyed it. It took me a while to learn how to but I have and it's that happiness which will carry me through the rest of my days. To have reached this point in my life I do truly feel that I am lucky.